This book is dedicated to:

Professor Sibte Jaffer
Servant of the Servants of Ali

The Grave of Ḥujr b. ʿAdī
Before and After the Terrorist Attack
on 2nd May 2013

What's your final wish before we execute you?

Hujr said: Kill my son first.

Why?

Kill my son, he said.

They executed his son.

He smiled.

Why do you smile they said?

He said: now I know my son died loving Ali I am ready to die.

I could not bear the thought that the sight of death may make him leave the love of Ali and become a lover of Muawiya.

I AM NOW READY TO DIE.

Hujr Ibn Adi al-Kindi

A Victim of Terror

by

Dr. Sayed Ammar Nakshawani

SAYED AMMAR PRESS

بسم الله الرحمن الرحيم

HUJR IBN ADI AL-KINDI

A VICTIM OF TERROR

by
Dr. Sayed Ammar Nakshawani

Published by Sayed Ammar Press
in association with Sun Behind The Cloud Publications Ltd
PO Box 15889, Birmingham, B16 6NZ

A CIP record of this title is available from the British Library

ISBN: 978-1-908110-18-3
Printed and bound in the UK

Front cover text quoted from: Ibn Kathīr, Ismāʿīl b. ʿUmar, *al-Bidāyah wa al-Nihāyah* (Beirut: Maktabah al-Maʿārif, 1966) The events of 51AH

Back cover text quoted from: al-Ṭabarī, Abū Jaʿfar Muḥammad b. Jarīr b.Yazīd, *The History of al-Tabari - Biographies of the Prophet's Companions and Their Successors*, vol 39, p274

Contents

About the Author	8
Acknowledgements	9
Foreword	11
Introduction	15
Ḥujr b. ʿAdī al-Kindī: A Victim of Terror	27
The Role of Muʿāwiya b. Abī Sufyān	35
Muʿāwiya's Treatment of Rebellions	47
The Execution of Ḥujr b. ʿAdī	53
Analysis of the Incident	67
Bibliography	72
Appendix	105

About the Author

Dr. Sayed Ammar Nakshawani is regarded as one of the most powerful speakers in the Muslim world. He was born in 1981 and graduated from the University College London, as well as the London School of Economics. He was then awarded with an MA in Islamic Studies from Shahid Beheshti University in Iran. Dr. Nakshawani completed his PhD thesis at the University of Exeter. He has lectured at the university in Classical Islamic History and then pursued further studies at the Islamic Seminary in Damascus, Syria. Currently he is a visiting scholar at the Centre of Islamic Studies, University of Cambridge.

Acknowledgments

My sincere gratitude goes to Kawther Rahmani, who edited this book through cancer out of her love for Ḥujr b. ʿAdī, and to all those who helped, supported and contributed to this work.

My special thanks extend to Yahya Seymour and Nader Zaveri for their research assistance; to Tehseen Merali of Sun Behind The Cloud Publications for her help in publishing the work; to al-Hajj Salman and Zain Moloobhoy for the unswerving support they have shown; to Dr Liaket Dewji and Hyderi Islamic Centre for the inspiration to write about this great man; to team SAN for their continued help, and to my family for instilling love of Ḥujr b. ʿAdī in my heart.

Your rewards are with the Almighty.

Foreword

Some analysts of the contemporary Middle East are far too quick to trace back current conflicts to ancient and long lasting hatreds. But sectarianism - and particularly pernicious forms of anti-Shīʿī feeling that seem rampant in the post-2003 world - has political causes, symptoms and consequences. However, history in the consciousness of many Muslims is not a dispassionate view of the past or even simply determined by our current preconceptions. Rather, history is the unfolding of the sacred intervening in the human; the events of the time of the Prophet and of the early communities constitute both the sacred history and the political theology that many believers hold to this day. Symbols matter whether they unite or divide. And personages are often the most powerful symbols.

Ḥujr b. ʿAdī was precisely one prominent figure - a companion of the Prophet, confidant of Imam ʿAlī, scourge of Muʿāwiya - who remains a potent symbol of dissent, as a model who spoke truth to power, whose identity has in the sectarianised conflict of contemporary Syria became a symbol of Shīʿī identity - despite and perhaps precisely because he was a common symbol before the hostilities of 2011. I remember visiting his shrine many times and being struck with the simple observation that this was a sacred space, a votive sanctuary that are common to all and particularly revered by the local Sunni inhabitants of the area in the hinterland of Damascus.

The brutal desecration of his tomb in Adhra, whilst being the result of a morally and intellectually bankrupt theology that has wrecked havoc in Arabia and also more recently in Mali, is more than just a disapproval of local expressions of spirituality or the covenants of pilgrimage and shrine visitation; it is a wilful act of provocation, an attack on what is perceived to be an exclusive repository of Shii identity.

This short and useful book, to which I am happy to add a few words by way of introduction and endorsement, demonstrates not only how the very historiography and visions of early sacred history continues to affect our world but also how Ḥujr b. ʿAdī's life and martyrdom expressed forms of Shīʿī identity in the Umayyad period as one finds present in the historical sources. The destruction of his shrine raises the question of who he was and what he means.

In answering such interrogations, Dr Sayed Ammar makes it clear how Ḥujr b. ʿAdī, while being a Shīʿī hero, should also be viewed as the Muslim exemplar, one who speaks for the values of social justice, the noble virtues of standing for the truths of faith and love against oppression, and being a faithful and true friend of ʿAlī b. Abī Tālib.

The current conflict around the world is for the very nature and understanding of Islam. By espousing and commemorating Hujr, believers can stand up for a conception of the faith that not only espouses universal values but seeks to promote human flourishing and achievement, in opposition to a distorted conception of Islam that reduces religiosity to nihilistic political action, destruction and murder.

We often learn through stories - we seem hard wired to enjoy narrative - and through the recollection of the case of Ḥujr b. ʿAdī

Dr Sayed Ammar contributes to a deeply felt and intentioned desire to say no to nihilism, to terrorism and to the wanton abuse of the faith, of Islam that so many millions of people hold dear just as they deeply love the symbols of that faith of love and human flourishing such as the Prophet, Imam ʿAlī, and their loved ones like Ḥujr b. ʿAdī.

Professor Sajjad H. Rizvi
MA, M.Phil (Oxon), Ph.D. (Cantab)
Associate Professor of Islamic Intellectual History
Institute of Arab and Islamic Studies
University of Exeter
June 2013

Introduction

'I came to say a word and I shall say it now, but if death prevents my word it will be said by tomorrow. For tomorrow never leaves a word unspoken'.

– Khalīl Gibrān

This work is dedicated to Ḥujr b. ʿAdī, the revered companion of Prophet Muḥammad (PBUH). A colossal figure in Islamic history, very much underestimated, understudied and undervalued. Arab historians are of the belief that Muʿāwiya was at fault for killing Ḥujr, and that Ḥujr and his supporters were innocent.[1] Some scholars believe that Ḥujr was oppressed by Zīyād and that Zīyād helped Muʿāwiya in making his decision to execute Ḥujr.[2] Shaʿbān viewed the act as that of a despot.

1. Muḥammad al-Sayyid al-Wakīl, *al-Umawīyyun bayn al-sharq wal-gharb; dirāsa wasfīyyah wa-taḥlīlīyya li-l-dawla al-Umawīyyah* (Damascus: Dar al-Qalam, 1995), 87-90; Muḥammad al-Ṭayyib al-Najjār, *al-Dawla al-Umawiyyah fi-l-sharq; bayna ʿawamil al-bina' wa-maʿawil al-fana* (Cairo: Dar al-Iʿtisam, 3rd edn., 1977), 80.

2. Ibrahīm Aḥmad al-ʿAdawī, *al-Dawla al-Umawiyyah* (Cairo: Maktabat al-Shabāb, 1987-88), 87; Muḥammad Mahir Hamda, *Dirāsa wathaiqiyya li-l-Tārīkh al-islamī wa-maṣadirihī; min ʿahd banī umayyah ḥata al-fatḥ al-ʿUthmānī li-Sūriyah wa-miṣr* 40-922AH /661-1516 C.E. (Beirut: Mu'assassat al Risāla, 1988), 38-39.

However, this victim of terror in his own lifetime was to also become a victim of terror after his death. The desecration of the grave of Ḥujr b. ʿAdī (AS), left me in a state of shock as well as frustration. I was truly flabbergasted at how low the human being can sink. I used to seek to visit his shrine every Friday when I was studying in the Islamic Seminary in Damascus. Memories came flooding back of tranquil moments of contemplation sitting next to this bastion of Islamic thought, bravery, valour and sacrifice. I remember the lectures I had given there, reflecting on his stand against the despotic terrorist of his time, Muʿāwiya I. I was astonished at what drives a human to seek to exhume the corpse of another human being. A theological edict, an unswerving loyalty to a cause, frustration, or poverty? Whatever it may be, to seek to desecrate the shrine of a fellow human being, irrespective of whatever their denomination or theological conclusion, is somewhat remarkable to say the least. Who would perform such an act of terror? For this behaviour is surely not befitting of any human being, surely not befitting of any Muslim. For a Muslim is taught to not only respect the body of a fellow Muslim, but to respect the sanctity of a fellow human being and the honour of a member of their community at large. A Muslim is taught to honour Prophet Muḥammad and those he loved. And Prophet Muḥammad (PBUH) loved Ḥujr.

There is not a day that goes by without a headline using the word terrorism. Televisions, radio, and print media alike are fixated with the employment of this term, highlighting what really is a bleak period in human history. From 9/11 to 7/7, Madrid or Boston, Oklahoma or Kerbala, Woolwich or Damascus, is anybody really safe from an attack on their lives involving a suicide bomber or a student depressed with what surrounds them? Many people are nervous at the sight of a mere backpack, let alone a face somewhat similar to those featured in posters of the FBI's Most Wanted. Many ask the question, can we not live in harmony with one another, co-exist in peace, tolerate our differences and build healthy community relationships on the basis of our similarities? Indeed, Khalīl Gibrān's words still echo the truth that 'we are all like the bright moon, [though] we still have our darker side', but surely not to this extent.

Terrorism, in the eyes of many today, is an act performed by a Muslim against a non-Muslim, but what people need to realise is that Muslims are also victims of terrorism at the hands of other Muslims. In its true meaning, being a Muslim and a terrorist is a paradox as Islam never condones such barbaric behaviour. It is indeed ironic when many assume that Islam and its followers are only terrorists and are never the victims of terrorism. The desecration of the grave of Ḥujr b. ʿAdī in Syria serves to highlight the fact that it is not only the non-Muslim who should be weary of terror, but even the Muslim whose theological conclusions are not in agreement with another Muslim may eventually be the victim of an attack. Unfortunately, this is not something new in the history of Islam. Just because some people call themselves Muslims does not mean that they follow the principles and ideals of the religion. A mere glance at our history will show that Islamic terrorism has always existed.

Fāṭima, the daughter of Prophet Muḥammad (PBUH), asked to be buried in the middle of the night, highlighting the existence of Muslim state terror in her time. Imam ʿAlī's burial site was not known until nearly one hundred years after his death out of fear that the terrorists of the time, known as Khārijites, would exhume his corpse. Abū Bakr's son Muḥammad was not only killed by fellow Muslims, but his body was placed in the corpse of a donkey and then set on fire. Ḥussain, the grandson of Prophet Muḥammad (PBUH), was beheaded by Muslim terrorists in Kerbala upon the orders of the terrorist Muslim caliph, Yazīd. Zayd, the great-grandson of Prophet Muḥammad (PBUH), has his nude body hung on a tree by the Umayyad state terror police. The Abbasids had prisons in different parts of Iraq ready to victimize and torture those who would just happen to disagree with their ways. The list could go on and on.

However, one would expect a certain amount of respect for a burial ground. While the dead have indeed moved on, their bodies should not be mutilated. They are to be judged by their Lord. Their good deeds are to be remembered. Visiting their graves is a lesson for everyone. According to verse 21 of Sūrat al-Kahf, when the Companions of the Cave went to sleep again, the people differed with one another on how to mark the place where they had gone to sleep, and they finally agreed to build a place of worship so that visitors, apart from visiting, could also engage in worshipping God. It is thus recorded in history books that every year the Prophet (PBUH) would visit the graves of the martyrs of the Battle of Uhud and recite this prayer: 'Peace be upon you because you were so constant; how excellent is then the issue of the abode?'

It is also recorded that Abū Bakr, ʿUmar and ʿUthmān, like the Prophet (PBUH), also used to perform such a visitation. Fāṭima, the daughter of the Prophet of Islam (PBUH), would also visit the martyrs of Uhud two days a week. During his visit to the martyrs, especially to Hamza and Muṣʿab b. ʿUmayr, the Holy Prophet (PBUH) would recite the following verse: 'Men who fulfill what they have pledged to Allāh' (33:23). In addition to this, Abū Saʿīd al-Khudrī would extend salutations to the grave of Hamza. Umm Salamah, one of the honorable wives of the Prophet (PBUH), and individuals such as Abū Hurayra, Fāṭima Khuzāʿīyya, and ʿAbd Allāh b. ʿUmar al-Khaṭṭāb also used to visit this group of martyrs. It is thus recorded in the important book, Al-Ghadīr, under the section, "Virtues and Merits of Abū Ḥānīfah" (Bab Fadāʿil wa Manaqib Abū Ḥānīfah) that whenever he would go to Baghdad, Imam ash-Shāfiʿī would pay a visit to the grave of Abū Ḥānīfah. He would stand beside his grave, offer salutation to him and seek his intercession for the fulfillment of his needs. Ahmad b. Ḥanbal did the same practice with respect to his master, Imam ash-Shāfi'ī, to such an extent that his son would get astonished.

This act of desecration stems from the ideology and propaganda of one region in the Muslim world, namely Saudi Arabia. In 1806, the Wahhabi terrorist army occupied Medina. They did not leave any religious building, including mosques, whether inside or outside the Baqī' (graveyard), without demolishing it. They intended to demolish the grave of the Prophet Muḥammad (PBUH) many times, but would repeatedly change their minds. At this time, non-Wahhabi Muslims were prevented from performing the Hajj (pilgrimage). In 1805, Iraqi and Iranian Muslims were refused permission to perform Hajj, as were the Syrians in 1806 and Egyptians the following year. The Saudi leader at the time wanted the pilgrims to embrace his Wahhabi beliefs and accept his mission. If they refused, he denied them permission to perform the Hajj and considered them to be heretics and infidels. The Wahhabi army's destruction campaign targeted the graves of the martyrs of Uhud, the mosque at the grave of Sayyid al-Shuhadā' Hamza b. 'Abdul Muṭṭalib and the mosques outside the Baqī': the Mosque of Fāṭima al-Zahra, the Mosque of al-Manāratayn, and Qubbat al-Thanayā (the burial site of the Prophet's (PBUH) incisor that was broken in the Battle of Uhud). The structures in the Baqī' were also leveled to the ground and not a single dome was left standing. This great place that was visited by millions of Muslims over many centuries became a garbage dump, such that it was not possible to recognize any grave or know whom it was for.

In 1818, the Wahhabis were defeated, and they withdrew from the holy places. The Prophet's (PBUH) Mosque, the Baqī' and the monuments at Uhud were rebuilt during the reigns of the Ottoman sultans 'Abd al-Majīd I, 'Abd al-Ḥamīd II and Maḥmūd II. From 1848 to 1860, the buildings were renovated and the Ottomans built the domes and mosques in splendid aesthetic style. They also rebuilt the Baqī' with a large dome over the graves of Imam Zainul ʿAbidīn (ʿAlī b. al-Ḥussain), Imam Muḥammad b. ʿAlī al-Bāqir and Imam Jaʿfar al-Sādiq. The graves of others related to the Prophet (PBUH) found at the Baqī' include those belonging to Ibrahīm (son), ʿUthmān b. ʿAffān (Companion and son-in-law), Ṣaffīyya bint ʿAbdul Muṭṭalib (aunt), ʿAtīka bint ʿAbd al-Muṭṭalib (aunt), Al-ʿAbbās b. ʿAbd al-Muṭṭalib (uncle), Fāṭima bint Asad (Imam ʿAlī's mother), ʿAbd Allāh b. Jaʿfar b. Abī Ṭālib (cousin) and Aqīl b. Abī Ṭālib (The Prophet's cousin).

The grave of the Prophet's (PBUH) father ʿAbd Allāh was in Dār al-Nābigha of the Banī Najjār, the house where the Prophet learned to swim. However, his father's grave was exhumed 17 years ago and transferred to the Baqī'. The area of the house today lies under the marble covering the plaza surrounding the mosque.

A number of the Prophet's (PBUH) wives (the Mothers of the Faithful) were buried in the Baqī': ʿAʿisha, Ḥafṣa, Jūwayrīyya, Ṣaffīyya, Sawda, Zaynab bint Khuzaima, Zaynab bint Jaḥsh, Umm Ḥabība and Umm Salama. The tomb of Khadīja, the Prophet's first wife, is in Mecca because she died before the Hijra (the migration of Muslims to Medina). Her grave is in the Ḥajūn cemetery, known as Maqbarat al-Maʿlā. The tomb of Maimouna, another wife, is also in Mecca in an area known as Sarīf, which lies on the side of the Hijra Road, nearly 13 miles (20 kilometers) outside of Mecca.

On 21st April 1925, the domes in the Baqī' were demolished once more along with the tombs of the holy personalities in Maqbarat al-Maʿlā in Mecca, where the Holy Prophet's (PBUH) mother, his wife Khadīja, grandfather and other ancestors are buried. The destruction of the sacred sites in the Ḥijāz continues till this day. Wahhabis say they are trying to rescue Islam from what they consider to be innovations, deviances and idolatries. Among the practices they believe are contrary to Islam are constructing elaborate monuments over graves and making supplications there. The Mashrubat Umm Ibrahīm - which was built to mark the location of the house where the Prophet's son, Ibrahīm, was born to Mārīah, his Egyptian wife - also contained the grave of Ḥamīda al-Barbarīyya, the mother of Imam Mūsā al-Kāzim. These sites were destroyed over the past few years.

When Muqbil b. Hādī al-Wadīʿī was a student at the University of Medina, he wrote a thesis entitled, About the Dome Built over the Grave of the Messenger, sponsored by Sheikh Ḥammād al-Anṣārī. In this paper, he demands that the noble grave be brought out of the Mosque. He says the presence of the holy grave and noble dome are major innovations and that they both need to be destroyed! His thesis received very high marks. A few years ago, the city planning board of Medina painted the famous green dome of the Prophet's (PBUH) Holy Mosque silver. After intense protests by the citizens of Medina, the board restored the dome to its original color.

In the Ottoman part of the Prophet's (PBUH) Mosque, at the center of the three sections, and raised a bit from the ground level, are three circles. The first, toward the west, corresponds to the grave of the Prophet (PBUH). The next two, toward the east, correspond to the graves of Abū Bakr and ʿUmar b. al-Khaṭṭab. Above the circles are invocations, such as 'Yā Allāh' and 'Yā Muḥammad'. The latter was removed and replaced with 'Yā Majīd' by adding the dot under the 'ḥā' of Muḥammad (PBUH) to make it 'jīm' and two dots under the second 'mīm' of Muḥammad (PBUH) to make it 'yā'. There are qaṣīdas written by rulers of the Muslim world, such as Sulṭān 'Abd al-Ḥamīd. Many verses of the famous Burda of al-Busīrī have also been painted over. On the Qibla side, the brass partition that is divided into three sections between two columns, the authorities have also tried to cover the famous two verses inscribed in the east from the story of al-ʿUtbī as mentioned by Ibn Kathīr in his tafsīr.

O best of those whose bones are buried in the deep earth,
and from whose fragrance the depth and height have become
sweet! May I be the ransom for a grave in which you dwell,
where purity, bounty and munificence [lives].

In 1998 the grave of ʿAmina bint Wahb, the Prophet's (PBUH) mother, was bulldozed in ʿAbwā and gasoline was poured over it. Even though thousands of petitions throughout the Muslim world were sent to Saudi Arabia, nothing could stop this heinous action from being performed. The House of Khadīja was excavated during the Haram extensions, then hurriedly covered over so as to obliterate any trace of it. This was the house where the Prophet (PBUH) received some of his first revelations and it is also where his children Umm Kulthūm, Ruqqaya, Zaynab, Fāṭima, and Qāsim were born. Dār al-Arqam, the first school in Islam where the Prophet taught, has also been demolished. It was in the area of Shiʿb ʿAlī near the Bāb ʿAlī door opposite the king's palace. It is now part of the extension of the Haram. The authorities plan to demolish the house of Mawlid, where the Prophet (PBUH) was born.

About 60 years ago, this house, which used to have a dome over it, was turned into a cattle market. Some people then worked together to transform it into a library, which it is today. It is lined with shelves of books about Mecca, most of them written by Meccans. But the library is under threat again because of the new Jabal ʿUmar project, one of the largest real estate development projects near the Grand Mosque. The birthplace of the Prophet (PBUH) is to make way for a car park and hotels. About 99% of real estate owners in the Jabal 'Umar area are shareholders in this company. The owners have been provided with financial incentives, including what they used to receive as rents, combining five-star facilities under the luxurious Le Meridien banner. The Meridien Towers will allow several thousand housing units in Mecca to be available during specified periods of time, for a one-off, fixed fee, giving the towers 25 years of shared ownership in Mecca. This scheme allow outsiders, whether Muslim or not, to invest in the city; they will be allowed to buy from a range of properties that can be used, sublet, resold or given as a gift.

In Medina, of the seven mosques at the site of the Battle of the Trench (Jabal al-Khandaq), where Sūrat al-Ahzāb was revealed, only two remain. The others have been demolished and a Saudi bank's cashpoint machine has been built in the area. The remaining mosques will be demolished as soon as the new mosque being constructed is ready. One of the mosques slated for destruction is Masjid Fatḥ, the mosque and rock of victory where the Prophet (PBUH) stood during the Battle of the Trench praying for victory. On the rock is where he received God's promises of victory and of the conquest of Mecca.

This study therefore will seek to historically examine the life and death of Ḥujr b. ʿAdī. It seeks to understand who Ḥujr b. ʿAdī *really* was, and why he and his companions were killed so mercilessly by Muʿāwiya. In brief, Wellhausen and Hawting portray Muʿāwiya as having little choice but to kill Ḥujr b. ʿAdī because of the schism that existed between Ḥujr and Zīyād and his only choice surprisingly, was to execute Ḥujr and forgive the latter.[1] Maḥmūd Ibrahīm concludes that Ḥujr was a threat to Muʿāwiya's economic interests, and therefore had to be executed, which is in line with Shaʿbān's 'despot' conclusion. The taking of the Ṣawafī land was the first step:

> With its income taken away from them, this faction of the New Segment were reduced further despite their objections

---

1. Julius Wellhausen, *The Religio-Political Factions of Early Islam*, ed. R.C. Ostle, trans. R.C. Ostle and S.M. Waltzer (Amsterdam-North Holland Publishing, 1975).

> which ended in the execution of Ḥujr b. ʿAdī and some of his supporters, the first political execution in Islam.[1]

Interesting to note that Hodgson believed that *ḥilm* was represented by executing those who were dividing the state. In executing Ḥujr, Hodgson views Muʿāwiya as the Arab-Shaykh and not an autocrat and that the unity of the Muslim community at the time could only be maintained by executing those who were deemed as threats, irrespective of their backgrounds or past service to the religion. Khaled Keshk concludes that the core of the Ḥujr incident is true, but that historians sought to add their own explanations within the narrative. He examines Ḥujr as the dissident and as the martyr, then analyses the different versions which portray his struggles with Muʿāwiya. Keshk seeks to portray that the inclusion of Khubayb b. ʿAdī in Baṣran sources sought to highlight how history repeats itself, as Abū Sufyān was a witness to Khabab's death and his son was a witness to Ḥujr's.[2] Such incidents would be included in narratives of other clashes to add weight to the image of the martyr, as discussed by Waldman and al-Qāḍī.[3]

By analyzing the life of this great companion of the Prophet Muḥammad (PBUH), we are able to see a distinct Shīʿī identity/theology in the formative period of Islamic History. Ḥujr's execution, in my opinion, is arguably one of the clearest proofs that a party who believed in the designation of ʿAlī by the Prophet (PBUH) are present and existed very early, and not as some would like to por-

1. Ibrahīm M. *The Social and Economic Background of the Umayyad Caliphate*, 370-1.

2. Keskh K. "The Historiography of an Execution: The Killing of Ḥujr b. ʿAdī", *Journal of Islamic Studies*, vol. 19, no. 1 (January 2008), 1-35.

3. Walmand M R. *Toward a Theory of Historical Narrative* (Columbus: Ohio State University Press, 1980); al-Qāḍī, W. *Bishr b. Kubar al-Balawī; namudhaj min al-nathr al-fanni al-mubakkir fi al-Yaman* (Beirut: Dār al-Gharb al-Islāmī, 1985)

tray as being a group whose beliefs were crystallized centuries later. Thirdly, we are able to reflect on our lives and seek to apply the lessons from his magnificent stands and principles today. How much have we truly sacrificed in our lives for the cause of the religion of Islam? How much have we sought to protect the tenets of the religion? How much have we sought to stand against the Muʿāwiya's of our time, representatives of tyranny, cruelty and hypocrisy in all it's forms? Ḥujr's grave may have been destroyed, but the terrorists can never obliterate his stands and principles from the heart's of the people. The words of Hind, the daughter of Zayd al-Anṣārī, recited to bewail Ḥujr, reverberate in the heart of every devout believer:

> O bright moon, go higher
> So that you may see Ḥujr walking!
> He is walking to Muʿāwiya b. Harb.
> (Muʿāwiya will) kill him as the Emīr has claimed.
> (He will) hang him on the gate of Damascus.
> So the eagles will eat from his charms.
> The tyrants have become haughty after Ḥujr.
> Al-Khwarnaq and al-Sidir (two palaces) have delighted them.
> The country has become faded
> As if no rain had enlivened it.
> O Ḥujr, Ḥujr b. ʿAdī,
> May safety and joy receive you.
> I fear that you will be killed as ʿAlī had been killed.
> If you perish, then every chief of people
> moves from this world to destruction.

Dr. Sayed Ammar Nakshawani
London, England
5th June 2013

Ḥujr b. ʿAdī al-Kindī: A Victim of Terror

Once Mecca had been conquered, a great number of pagan tribes became Muslim of their own accord, whereas others accepted Islam when the Prophet sent missionaries to instruct people in the tenets of the Muslim religion. ʿAlī b. Abī Tālib was one of the Prophet's companions who was sent to Yemen in 10 AH to invite the Yemeni tribes to Islam. His efforts had a monumental affect on many of the youths in that region as well as endearing him to many of them forever. Although the final expedition which the Prophet organized was under the command of Usāma b. Zayd b. Ḥāritha on the Syrian frontier, he never left Medina in his lifetime. Accordingly, the missionary expedition to Yemen in Ramadhan 10 AH under the command of ʿAlī was the last one which left the city of Medina while he was still alive.

The army arrived with ʿAlī in the winter period, and he begun to invite the leaders of Madhḥaj to accept Islam. Their reply was a unanimous score of arrows and rocks whereupon he also signaled his troops to charge. They attacked the tribesmen and routed them but did not pursue them because ʿAlī's mission was one of peace and not of war. His orders to his troops were to fight only in self-defense. The Madhḥaj wanted peace which ʿAlī granted them, and he renewed his invitation to them to accept Islam. This time they and also the tribe of Ḥamdān responded to his call, and accepted Islam. The whole of

Yemen became Muslim through the efforts of ʿAlī .

The tribe of Kinda belonged to the band of Kahlān, and their homeland was Yemen. Many of their leaders then moved to Iraq. Kahlān and Ḥimyar were the two sons of Saba'; this was the name which brought both tribes together. It was said: 'The Arabs regarded the houses with glory and honor after the house of Hāshim b. ʿAbd Manāf as four houses. They were the house of Qays al-Fāzāzī, (the house of) the Darīmīyyīn, (the house of) Band Shayn, and the house of Yemen, who belonged to the bane of al-Ḥarith b. Kaʿb'. As for the Kinda, they were not regarded simply as ordinary people from the houses. They were kings, and among them was al-Malik al-Dilīl (i.e., ʿUmrū' al-Qays). They had authority in both Yemen and al-Ḥijāz. The glory of Kinda lasted during the time of Islam. A few of the Kindīs took part in the conquests and the revolts; while some of them were governors, others were judges, such as Ḥusayn b. Ḥasan al-Ḥujrī; and there were poets such as Jaʿfar b. ʿAffan al-Makfūf, the poet of the Shīʿa, in their lineage. Hānī b. al-Wad b. ʿAdī, the nephew of Ḥujr, was among the noble figures of Kūfah. Jaʿfar b. al Ashʿath and his son al-ʿAbbās b. Jaʿfar were among the Shīʿa of Imam Abū al-Ḥasan (i.e., Mūsā b. Jaʿfar) and his son al-Riḍa, peace be upon them. As for al-Ashʿath b. Qays al-Kindī, he was the greatest of all the hypocrites in Kūfah. He became Muslim, then he renounced Islam after the Prophet died. Then he became Muslim, and Abū Bakr accepted his Islam. Abū Bakr then married him to his sister who was the mother of Muḥammad b. al-Ashʿath. Imam al-Ḥasan married al-Ashʿath's daughter whom Muʿāwiya asked to give poison for Imam al-Ḥasan to drink.

Ḥujr b. ʿAdī's full name was Ḥujr b. ʿAdī b. Jabāl b. ʿAdī b. Rābiʿah b. Muʿāwiya al-Akbār b. al-Ḥārith b. Muʿāwiya b. Thawr b. Bazīgh b. Kindī al-Kūfī. He was known as Ḥujr al-Khayr (Ḥujr the Good). There is a difference of opinion as to whether Ḥujr was a companion or from the followers of the companions as he is included in the lists of both groupings, however in his book *Al-Mustadrak*, al-Ḥakim has described him as 'the monk of the Companions of Muḥammad, may Allāh bless him and his family'.[1]

He fought in the Ridda and later took part in the battle of al-Qādisīyyah on the Sasanian front.[2] He fought alongside ʿAlī b. Abū Ṭālib in the Battles of the Camel and Ṣiffīn and was one of his staunch supporters.[3] Ḥujr and his brother Hānī b. ʿAdī came to the Prophet, may Allāh bless him and his family. In his book *Al-Istīʿāb* , Ibn ʿAbd al-Birr al-Malikī said, 'Ḥujr was among the excellent companions, and his age was less than their old ones'. In his book *Asad al-Ghāba*, Ibn al-Athīr has mentioned him with words similar to these .

Imam ʿAlī attracted more Shīʿa from the ʿAdnānī tribes than from among the Qaḥṭānī ones; although Shīʿism among the Qaḥṭānīs had grown a great deal as well. The principal Shīʿa who comprised the soldiers and compilers of history of the Commander of the Faithful were Arab tribes from Yemen in the south and and from among the Qaḥṭānīs. For example, Imam ʿAlī said in Rājzī, one of the battle arenas in Ṣiffīn:

أنا الغلام القرشي المؤتمن الماجد الأبيض ليث كالشّطن

يرضى به السّادة من اهل اليمن من ساكني نجد و من اهل عدن

1. al-Nīsābūrī, Muḥammad b. ʿAbd Allāh al-Ḥakīm, *al-Mustadrak ala l-Ṣaḥīḥayn* (India: Dā'irat al-Maʿārif al-Nād'imiyet al-Qā'ima fī l-Hind, 1913).

2. Ibn Saʿd, *Al-Ṭabaqāt*, vol. 6, 151.

3. Ibn Kathīr, *Al-Bidāya wa-l-Nihāya*, ed. ʿAlī ʿAbd al-Sātir (Beirut: Dar al-Kutub al-ʿIlmīyyah, 1985), vol. 3, 51-2.

> I am a Qurayshī youth — trustworthy, great, pure, and like a lion — with whom the distinguished men of the people of Yemen from among the residents of Najd and ʿAden are pleased.[1]

Likewise, after the death of the Prophet of Islam (PBUH), the majority of ʿAlī's followers from among the companions of the Prophet (PBUH) were Anṣār whose origins were Qaḥṭānī. It was most of these men who had accompanied ʿAlī from Medina to the Battle of Jamal.[2] Similarly, when Imam al-Ḥusayn set off toward Kūfah, ʿAbd Allāh b. al-ʿAbbās said to him:

> If the people of Iraq like you and want to assist you, you write to them, "The enemy shall expel you from your city. Then, you come here." Instead, you move toward Yemen where there are mountains, strongholds and forts that Iraq does not have. Yemen is a vast land and your father have Shīʿa there. You go there and then send your preachers to the neighboring places to invite the people to come to you.

The companions of Imam al-Ḥusayn, with the exception of Banū Hāshim and a few Ghaffārīs, belonged to tribes from Yemen as well. As Masʿūdī has said, 'From among the companions of the Prophet (PBUH), only four persons attained martyrdom at the lap of the Prophet (S) and these four were from the Anṣār'.[3]

1. Ibn Shāhrashūb Māzandarānī, *Manāqib Al Abī Ṭālib* (Qum: Muʿassasah Intisharat-e ʿAllameh, n.d.), vol. 3, 178.

2. Aḥmad b. Yaḥyā b. Jābir Balādhurī, *Ansāb al-Ashrāf*, researched by Muḥammad Bāqir Maḥmūdī (Beirut: Manshurat Muʿassasah al-Aʿlami Li'l-Matbuʿat, 1394 AH), vol. 3, 161.

3. ʿAlī b. Ḥusayn b. ʿAlī Masʿūdī, *Murūj al-Dhahāb wa Maʿādin al-Jawhar*, 1st edition (Beirut: Manshurat Muʿassasah al-Aʿlamī Li'l-Matbuʿat, 1411 AH), vol. 3, 84

After the Battle of Nahrawān, Muʿāwiya sent Al-Ḍaḥḥāk b. Qays al-Fihrī with a force of four thousand towards Kūfah with the purpose that he should create disorder in this area, kill whomever he finds and keep busy in bloodshed and destruction so that Amīr al-Muʿminīn should find no rest or peace of mind. He set off for the achievement of this aim, and shedding innocent blood and spreading destruction all round reached up to the place of al-Thaʿlabīyyah. Here he attacked a caravan of pilgrims (to Mecca) and looted all their wealth and belongings. Then at al-Quṭquṭānah he killed the nephew of ʿAbdullāh b. Masʿūd, the Holy Prophet's companion, namely, ʿAmr b. ʿUways b. Masʿud together with his followers. In this manner he created havoc and bloodshed all round. When Amīr al-Muʿminīn came to know of this rack and ruin he called his men to battle in order to put a stop to this vandalism, but people seemed to avoid war. Being disgusted with their lethargy and lack of enthusiasm he ascended the pulpit and delivered this sermon, wherein he has roused the men to feel shame and not to try to avoid war but to rise for the protection of their country like brave men without employing wrong and lame excuses. At last Ḥujr b. ʿAdī al-Kindī rose with a force of four thousand for crushing the enemy and overtook him at Tadmur. Only a small encounter had taken place between the parties when night came on and he fled away with only nineteen killed on his side. In the army two persons also fell as martyrs. This sermon in the Nahj al-Balāgha sets the scene:

> O people, your bodies are together but your desires are divergent. Your talk softens the hard stones and your action attracts your enemy towards you. You claim in your sittings that you would do this and that, but when fighting approaches, you say (to war), 'turn thou away' (i.e. flee away). If one calls you (for help) the call receives no heed. And he who deals hardly with you his heart has no solace. The excuses are amiss

> like that of a debtor unwilling to pay. The ignoble can not ward off oppression. Right cannot be achieved without effort. Which is the house besides this one to protect? And with which leader (Imam) would you go for fighting after me?
>
> By Allāh! Deceived is one whom you have deceived while, by Allāh! he who is successful with you receives only useless arrows. You are like broken arrows thrown over the enemy. By Allāh! I am now in the position that I neither confirm your views nor hope for your support, nor challenge the enemy through you. What is the matter with you? What is your ailment? What is your cure? The other party is also men of your shape (but they are so different in character). Will there be talk without action, carelessness without piety and greed in things not right?![1]

Furthermore, on the night of the assassination Ibn Muljam came to al-Ashʿath b. Qays and both retired to a corner of the mosque and sat there when Ḥujr b. ʿAdī passed by and he heard al-Ashʿath saying to Ibn Muljam, 'Be quick now or else dawn's light would disgrace you'. On hearing this Ḥujr said to al-Ashʿath, 'O one-eyed man, you are preparing to kill ʿAlī' and hastened towards ʿAlī b. Abī Ṭālib, but Ibn Muljam had preceded him and struck ʿAlī with his sword. When Ḥujr turned back, people were crying, 'Alī has been killed'.

Later, Al-Ḥasan sent Ḥujr b. ʿAdī to order the leaders to set out and to call the people together for war (jihād). They were slow to (answer) him and then they came forward. (Al-Ḥasan) had a mixed band of men: some of them belonged to his Shiʿa and to his father's; some of them were members of the Muḥakkima (i.e., Khārijites) who were influenced by (the desires of) fighting Muʿāwiya with every means (possible); some of them were men who loved discords and were anxious for booty; some of them were doubters; others were

1. Sermon 29, *Nahjul Balāgha*

tribal supporters who followed the leaders of their tribes without reference to religion'.

Al-Ḥasan, peace be on him, followed all these ways from the day when he assumed the succession in Kūfah. Also he used them when he declared jihād. Among his measures, as we have said earlier, were that he increased the salaries of the fighters a hundred percent. He sent Ḥujr b. ʿAdī to his rulers to summon them to jihād. His notable companions, who were orators, helped him with his task. Among them were ʿAdī b. Hātam, Maʿqal b. Qays al-Riyāḥī, Zīyīd b. Saʿsaʿa al-Tamīmī, and Qays b. Saʿd al-Anṣārī. They criticized the people for their slowness and urged them to take part in jihād for Allāh. Then they themselves competed with each other for their places in the general camp, and they competed with the people for that.

They spread the standards of jihād all over Kūfah. They summoned the people (to obey) Allāh, the Great and Almighty, and the family of Muḥammad, peace be on them. The partisans of ʿAlī revolted against Muʿāwiya and his central government. They had paid allegiance to al-Ḥasan, son of ʿAlī and grandson of Muḥammad, soon after the battle of Ṣiffīn and the murder of ʿAlī. They viewed al-Ḥasan as the legitimate successor to ʿAlī. Muʿāwiya did not believe that al-Ḥasan had the capability of leading and dismissed him, by stating:

> I admit that your blood relationship gives you a clear title to the office. If I knew that you were more capable than I in keeping the people under discipline, more considerate of this Ummah, a better statesman, more effective in collecting the revenues, and a greater deterrent against the enemy, I would certainly swear allegiance to you. But I have had long enough in this position and I have much more experience in its duties than you have.[1]

1. Al-Isfahānī, Abul Faraj, *Maqātil al-Ṭālibiyīn*, ed. Aḥmed Saqr, (Cairo, 1949), 2nd edition, (Tehran, 1970), 58.

The Role of Mu'āwiya b. Abī Sufyān

According to traditional Muslim sources, Mu'āwiya was born in Mecca five years before the open proclamation of the religion of Islam.[1] His father was Ṣakhr b. Ḥarb b. Umayyah b. 'Abd Shams b. 'Abd Manāf, who was known as Abū Sufyān and his mother was Hind bt. 'Utbah b. Rabī'ah b. 'Abd Shams b. 'Abd Manāf.[2] Abū Sufyān had two sons, Yazīd and Mu'āwiya, and a daughter named Umm Ḥabība. Mu'āwiya ruled the Islamic nascent Muslim community from 41-60/661-680. Historians see Mu'āwiya as either the first or the second of the Umayyad Caliphs as 'Uthmān b. 'Affān ruled before him from 23-35/644-656.[3] 'Uthmān is viewed as being amongst the

1. Aḥmad b. 'Alī Ibn Ḥajar al-'Asqalānī, *al-Iṣābah fī tamyīz al-ṣaḥābah* (Cairo: Būlāq, 1328/1910), vol. 3, 433.

2. On Abū Sufyān, see Abū 'Amr Khalīfa Ibn Khayyāṭ, *al-Ṭabaqāt: riwāyat Abī 'Imrān Mūsā al-Tustarī*, ed. Akram Ḍiyā' al-'Umarī (Baghdad: Maṭba'at al-'Ānī, 1967), 297; 'Abdullāh b. Muslim Ibn Qutayba, *Kitāb al-ma'arif*, ed. Tharwat 'Ukāshah (Cairo: Maṭba'at Dār al-Kutub, 1960), 344; 'Alī b. al-Ḥusayn al-Mas' ūdī, *al-Tanbīḥ wa-l-ishrāf* (Leiden, 1894, rpt., Beirut: Maktabat al-Khayyāṭ, 1965); on Hind, see Ibn Khayyāṭ, *al-Ṭabaqāt*, 298.

3. Asma Afsaruddin, *The First Muslims: History and Memory* (Oxford: Oneworld Publications, 2008), 47-50, discusses the notion of 'Uthmān as being amongst the Rightly Guided Caliphs. Cf. M. A. Shaban, *Islamic History: A New Interpretation A.D. 600-750* (Cambridge: Cambridge University Press, 1971), vol. 1, 63.

rightly guided Caliphs, an honour notably given to only one other Umayyad, ʿUmar II.[1] Muʿāwiya, however, is regarded as the founder of the Caliphate of the Umayyad dynasty.[2] The Sufyanid dynasty refers solely to Muʿāwiya and his lineage, which came to an end with the death of his grandson Muʿāwiya II in 64/683, thus marking the beginning of the Marwānid dynasty.

There is a difference of opinion on the timing of Muʿāwiya's conversion to Islam.[3] A conversion preceding the conquest of Mecca would be more favorable in light of later claims for the Caliphate, as he would not be categorized as being one of the freed ones, known as the *tulaqāh*. One narration discusses his conversion as taking place before the occupation of Mecca. The narration discusses the fact that he accepted Islam at the Treaty of Ḥudaybīyyah.[4] Another nar-

1. G.R. Hawting, *The First Dynasty of Islam* (London: Routledge, 2000), 18. It is not very clear when the term *al-Khulāfa' al-Rāshidūn* was crystallised. Afsaruddin comments on page 55 of *The First Muslims* that 'the concept began to crystallize at some point during the Umayyad period when, against the backdrop of what appeared to be a deliberate reversion to pre-Islamic values, nostalgia for the age of the Prophet and his Companions must have become pronounced. Abū Hanīfa (d. 767) and Aḥmed b. Hanbal (d. 855) are credited with being the earliest scholars to recognise the chronological order of the four *Rāshidūn* caliphs and to have imparted a certain degree of theological significance to this order'. There is a difference of opinion as to whether was ʿAlī was initially excluded from the list of caliphs. See Madelung, *The Succession to Muḥammad*, 173. This seems to have changed by the late eighth century. See M. Watt, *The Formative Period of Islamic Thought* (Edinburgh: Edinburgh University Press, 1973), 77.

2. Hawting, *The First Dynasty of Islam*, 1.

3. Ibn ʿAsākir, *Tārīkh Madīnat Dimashq*, ed. Muḥibb al-Dīn Abī Sa'īd 'Umar b. Gharāma al-'Amrawī (Beirut: Dār al-Fikr, 1995-1998) vol. 61, 57. See also al-Balādhurī, Ansāb al-Ashrāf, ed. Iḥsān 'Abbās (Wiesbaden: Franz Steiner, 1979), vol. 4, 13, who discusses a different though not exact date and indicates that it was earlier than the conquest of Mecca.

4. Ibn Ḥajar, *al-Iṣābah*, vol. 3, 433; see also I. Hasson, *JSAI*, 22 (1998), 'La conversion de Muʿāwiya b. Abī Sufyān', 219.

ration, however, indicates a conversion to Islam in the year 8 AH, hence counting him amongst the freedmen in Mecca.[1] After his conversion, Muʿāwiya was given one hundred camels and forty ounces of gold from the booty of the Battle of Ḥunayn, for he was one of those whose hearts had been reconciled.[2] Muʿāwiya was employed by the Prophet as a secretary,[3] or *kātib*.[4] Amongst his duties was to ensure messages were written to chiefs of different Arab tribes.[5]

Muʿāwiya served the state during the rule of the first three caliphs. First, he acted as lieutenant of the army that conquered Syria during the reign of Abū Bakr. Then, when Khālid b. Saʿīd b. al-Āṣ had been defeated and killed by the Byzantines in the Battle of Marj al-Ṣuffar in the year 13/633, Muʿāwiya was head of the 3, 000 tribesmen that were part of the expedition.[6] Furthermore, during the reign of ʿUmar,[7] he fought and defeated the Byzantines in the Battle of al-Yarmūk in 15/635 and would then continue under ʿUthmān as a military governor.[8]

The political divisions of the period between 656 and 661 acquired significance in regards to the discussions of Muʿāwiya's authority

1. Al-Ṭabarī, *Tārīkh al-Rusul wa'l-mulūk*, ed. M.J. de Goej, et al (Leiden: Brill, 1881), vol. 1, 1642-3.

2. Ismail b. ʿUmar Ibn Kathīr, *al-Bidāyah wa al-Nihāyah* (Beirut: Maktabah al Ma'ārif, 1966), vol. 8, 117.

3. Afsaruddin,*The First Muslims*, 81.

4. Izz al-Dīn Ibn al-Athīr, *al-Kāmil fi al-Tārīkh*, ed. C.J. Tornberg (Leiden: Brill, 1868-70), vol. 2, 313.

5. Ibn Ḥajar, *al-Iṣabah*, vol. 3, 434.

6. Al-Ṭabarī, *Tārīkh al-Rusul wa'l-mulūk*, vol. 1, 2090-1.

7. S. Bashear, "The Title Fārūq and its Association with ʿUmar I", *Studia Islamica*, 72 (1990), 47-70.

8. Aḥmed b. Yaḥyā al-Balādhurī, *Futūḥ al-Buldān*, ed. M. de Goeje (Leiden: Brill, 1865), 135-6. See also R.B. Serjeant, "The Caliph ʿUmar's Letters to Abū Musā and Muʿāwiya", *Semitic Studies*, 24 (1984), 65-79.

and leadership for later Muslims.[1] These events shaped the identities and political thoughts of Muslim communities.[2] Irreconcilable factions within the community were to be explained in light of the civil wars after the murder of ʿUthmān.[3] Tensions were clearly prevalent within the new Muslim community.[4] Old rivalries between the Meccans and Medinans, as well as inter-tribal conflicts, were revived. The newly created Islamic theocracy was full of dissensions.[5] Abū Bakr and ʿUmar were seen to have upheld a *modus vivendi*[6] with their recognition of the religious and political aspects of leading the Islamic state.[7] However, with the emergence of ʿUthmān and the Umayyads, dissatisfaction once again resurfaced.[8] Muʿāwiya's leadership is central to this period and its main events as we shall see.[9]

It is a period referred to by Donner as the era of 'Islamic origins'.[10]

---

1. M. Hinds, "The Murder of the Caliph ʿUthmān", *IJMES*, 3 (1972), 450-69.

2. M. Sharon, "Notes on the Question of Legitimacy of Government in Islam", *Israel Oriental Studies*, 10 (1980), 116-23.

3. P. Crone, *God's Rule* (New York: Columbia University Press, 2004), 23.

4. Hinds, "The Murder of the Caliph ʿUthmān".

5. G. Hawting, "The Significance of the Slogan *La Ḥukma illa Lillah* and the References to the *Ḥudūd* in the Traditions about the *Fitna* and the Murder of ʿUthmān", *BSOAS*, 41 (1978), 453-463.

6. E. Petersen, *'Alī and Mu'āwiya* (Copenhagen: Munksgaard, 1964), Introduction. However, Madelung questions the legitimacy of their authority in light of the events at Saqīfat Banī Sā'idah - see Madelung, *The Succession to Muḥammad*, 28.

7. W.M. Watt, "God's Caliph: Quranic Interpretations and Umayyad Claims", *Iran and Islam*, ed. C.E. Bosworth (Edinburgh: Edinburgh University Press, 1971).

8. Madelung, *The Succession to Muḥammad*, 113. See also M. Quṭb, *Social Justice In Islam*, tr. John Hardie (New York: Octagon Books, 1970), 183.

9. M. Sharon, "The Umayyads as Ahl al-Bayt", *Jerusalem Studies in Arabic and Islam*, 14 (1992), 115-52.

10. Donner, *Narratives of Islamic Origins*, 1.

The history of Islamic origins is mainly taken from the Islamic tradition itself. There are extensive sources for this - that fact is not under question.[1] Yet the documentary value of such sources is under intense scrutiny and this in many cases reduces the confidence of scholars when seeking to build a traditional picture of Islamic origins.[2] This is not to deny that there are sources which, although outside of the Islamic tradition, were contemporary with the spread of Islam.[3] These have been viewed as being more reliable than the Islamic sources, as they were produced without any type of theological or political stance underpinning the way history is portrayed.[4] These sources are of the utmost importance, though at times they may not provide conclusive or even helpful results in relation to certain parts of history.[5] Particular detail shall be paid in our study to the conditions for leadership, which are listed in such sources, in order to examine the reign of Muʿāwiya. 'The Maronite Chronicle', compiled by an anonymous Maronite Christian author, recorded Mu'āwiya's succession as caliph. This chronicle was compiled between 664 and 727 and is seen as a near contemporaneous source.[6] This is the view adopted by Marsham when he states:

---

1. M. Hinds, "The Siffin Arbitration Agreement", *JSS*, 17 (1972), 92-129.

2. S.P. Brock, "Syriac Sources for Seventh Century History", *Byzantine and Modern Greek Studies*, 2 (1976).

3. M. Lecker, "The Estates of ʿAmr b. al-Āṣ in Palestine: Notes on a New Negev Arabic Inscription", *BSOAS*, 52 (1989), 24-37.

4. W. Kaegi, "Initial Byzantine Reactions to the Arab Conquests", *Church History*, 38 (1969), 139-49; R. Hoyland, "Sebeos, the Jews and the Rise of Islam", *Studies in Muslim-Jewish Relations*, 2 (1996), 89-102.

5. F. Donner, *The Early Islamic Conquests* (Princeton: Princeton University Press, 1981), 142-146.

6. A. Palmer, S. Brock, and R. Hoyland, *The Seventh Century in the West-Syrian Chronicles* (Liverpool: Liverpool University Press, 1993), 29.

> The two Syriac accounts of Mu'āwiya's succession in Syria are not only contemporaneous evidence for early Umayyad succession ritual than anything in the extant Arabic-Islamic material but are also more detailed in many respects. We can be reasonably confident that they are near contemporaneous, even perhaps eyewitness accounts, copied by the compiler of the chronicle.[1]

The narratives indicate a ceremony representing a shift from the Caliphate to kingship. Muʿāwiya's reign as leader marks that shift from Caliphate to kingship in light of the conditions of leadership as stipulated in the sources.

A survey of the sources that discuss Muʿāwiya's leadership is therefore vital. Historical, theological, jurisprudential, adab and jurisprudence literature form the basis of the narratives relating to the period in and around the fitnah and provide adequate evidence that the theory of the schools can be rejected and that through source criticism, the similarities and contradictions in the narratives display no clear political or ideological motive in compilation.

While stressing the lack of sympathy within Shīʿī and Khārijite circles, Humphreys does admit that Muʿāwiya does not necessarily fall within the definition of the more traditional religious circles:

> The real problem is that he did not fit neatly into the moral categories which later Muslims decided to evaluate a person's religious standing - indeed, he subverted them, and so they could never quite decide what to make of him.[2]

---

1. A. Marsham, *Rituals of Islamic Monarchy, Accession and Succession in the First Muslim Empire* (Edinburgh: Edinburgh University Press, 2009), 87-88.

2. Humphreys, *Muʿāwiya b. Abī Sufyān*, 3.

He speaks of 'Arabic sources, dominated by Iraqi and pro-'Alid perspectives'.[1] 'Alī is portrayed here as never intending to find the killers of 'Uthmān. But at the same time, he ironically belittles Mu'āwiya's approach to events. First is the clear lack of help he offers his cousin in his time of need. Intrigue overshadows much of Mu'āwiya's intention for the position of Caliphate, like that of his partner 'Amr b. al-Āṣ, 'a man not above cynical opportunism'.[2]

Humphreys introduces certain members of the Caliph's government - people whose personal conduct had 'often been scandalous',[3] like al-Mughīrah and the hapless Zīyād, son of his father, named because of his mysterious, adulterous birth. 'To win the reluctant Zīyād to his cause, Mu'āwiya had the idea of proclaiming that he was the son of his own father Abū Sufyān'[4], an act of un-Islamic proportions. This Zīyād is highly praised by Humphreys, especially in a comical narration of his striking of an innocent bedouin's head![5] Humphreys does, however, admit that Mu'āwiya 'lacked and almost certainly never desired, the religious charisma of Muḥammad but in his methods of using political means for political ends, he is perhaps no different'.[6]

Moreover, the depiction of Mu'āwiya, according to Keshk, very much depends on the period in which the accounts have taken place and who the narrators of the respective events are. His work includes an analysis of some diametrically opposed depictions, within three periods, pre-civil war, civil war and post-civil war. In the pre-civil war period, Mu'āwiya's image is portrayed as that of an obedi-

1. Ibid, 79.
2. Ibid, 81.
3. Ibid, 86.
4. Ibid, 89.
5. Ibid, 92.
6. Ibid, 93.

ent governor. His loyalty, bravery and piety all emerge. What is the reasoning behind this? Keshk believes this is very much related to the fact that the historical tragedy of the first civil war had not yet affected Muʿāwiya's persona.[1]

Keshk then continues by looking at 'civil war Muʿāwiya' and discusses the fact that the negative images which emerge are due to parallels made between ʿAlī's struggle with Muʿāwiya and Muḥammad's struggle with Abū Sufyān.[2] Keshk then sheds light on two of the most important incidents in defining Muʿāwiya's image in Islamic history, the killing of Ḥujr b. ʿAdī al-Kindī and the appointment of Yazīd as heir apparent. Again, the question is raised, is Muʿāwiya the proverbial Arab sheikh or the despot? Keshk argues that this all depends on the way one views Ḥujr. Is Ḥujr a rebel against the cause or is he a renowned companion of the Prophet? Likewise, when discussing Yazīd, he analyses the regional and political factors that led to the appointment.[3]

Keshk's main point is that history and historiography are two different things. 'Madelung takes this argument, as he does with every negative comment about Muʿāwiya, with absolute truth. Although Madelung does seem to accept the story at face value, we believe he misses out some of its subtleties, or maybe he purposely avoids them'.[4] Again Keshk believes that without considering the sources and the environment of the time, Madelung is amongst the historians who have reached the wrong conclusions:

> Muʿāwiya and his followers were easily stigmatized by the simple injection of Muʿāwiya's name among the confederates

1. Keshk, *The Depiction of Muʿāwiya*, 18.
2. Ibid, 53.
3. Ibid, 101.
4. Ibid, 106.

> besieging Medina at the Battle of the Trench. This association remained with Muʿāwiya and his followers through their subsequent struggle with ʿAlī and his supporters. Indeed, Muʿāwiya's character in these depictions was that of an evil, irreligious, cowardly usurper who was unworthy of the support of other Muslims, let alone the caliphate. This re-working of Muʿāwiya's image has been sufficiently effective that one modern scholar, namely Madelung, has accepted it as a true reflection of a historical figure, rather than the fictional story telling of the classical Muslim historians.[1]

However, Keshk's conclusion is rejected when examining the sources and the way they depict Muʿāwiya's decisions. Keshk seeks to explain the killing of Ḥujr b. ʿAdī by proposing the theory that historians emphasize certain elements of the story of Ḥujr to highlight a particular political bias, and that when this is done, they are taking away from the fact that 'these sources had a primary purpose that was lost on modern scholars in their use of the Ḥujr story'. The reply, however, is that the emphasis on these elements was to portray a clearer understanding of the motives and the backgrounds of the execution. Historians are in agreement on four major parts of the narrative. The first is a discussion of the disagreement which occurred between Ḥujr, al-Mughīrah and Zīyād. The second is that they discuss the background to his disobedience of the authorities in Kūfah, the third is his arrest and the fourth is his execution. Keshk states that while they all agree, they tend to emphasize one incident over another. The emphasis of one incident over another does not hide the over-arching question as to whether Muʿāwiya's conclusive decision concerning Ḥujr was that of a *ḥalīm* or that of a *jāhil*.

---

1. Keshk, *The Depiction of Muʿāwiya*, 185.

Muʿāwiya's does not display *ḥilm* in his dealings with Ḥujr. It was a ruthless decision that was undertaken, with no tolerance or respect shown to the men who tried to intercede on behalf of Ḥujr. The offer to exile them into different parts of the empire would no doubt have silenced his critics and the critics of Zīyād as well. But the government had reached a stage where dissidents were not tolerated, especially those who continued to display love towards ʿAlī, his family and their political beliefs. In each case, Shaban concludes that Muʿāwiya acts as a despot in his dealings with Ḥujr.[1]

This point is stressed upon by Quṭb. While Quṭb may not be regarded as a historian as such, his later social influence in Islamic political circles is very clear.[2] Quṭb is extremely critical of the sources that depict Muʿāwiya as being of the earlier entourage of companions and a man of known piety. Muʿāwiya's biography and subsequent credentials are examined and he disagrees with the picture portrayed by some historians:

> The erroneous fable still persists that Muʿāwiya was a scribe who wrote down the revelations of Allāh's Messenger. The truth is that when Abū Sufyān embraced Islam, he besought the Prophet to give Muʿāwiya some measure of position in the eyes of the Arabs; thus he would be compensated of being slow to embrace Islam and of being one of those who had no precedence in the new religion. So the Prophet used Muʿāwiya for writing letters and contracts and agreements. But none

1. Shaban, *Islamic History*, 89.

2. W. Shepard, "The Development of the Thought of Sayyid Quṭb as Reflected in Earlier and Later Editions of 'Social Justice in Islam'", *Die Welt des Islam*, 32 (1992); See also W. Shepard, "Sayyed Quṭb's Doctrine of Jahilīyya", *IJMES*, 35 (2003), 521-45.

> of the companions ever said that he wrote down any of the Prophet's revelations, as was asserted by Mu'āwiya's partisans after he had assumed the throne.[1]

Yet no historian of the modern school has been as scathing in his attack on the Umayyads in general and Mu'āwiya in particular as Madelung:

> The cancer in the body of the caliphate which had nurtured and proved unable to excise because of his doting love for a corrupt and rapacious kin destroyed him. It was to continue to grow and to sweep away 'Umar's caliphate of the Islamic meritocracy. 'Uthmān's successor, Mu'āwiya, turned it, as predicted by a well-known prophecy ascribed to Muḥammad, into traditional despotic kingship.[2]

This view of Mu'āwiya, in stark contrast to Humphreys and others, is further emphasized in discussing what they he viewed as *ḥilm*:

> Mu'āwiya had developed a taste for despotism of the Roman Byzantine type. While endowed with a natural instinct for power and domination, his judgment of human nature was, contrary to his reputation, limited and primitive. He had come to understand that in statecraft, whenever bribery or intimidation would not reduce an opponent, murder, open or secret, was the most convenient and effective means.[3]

---

1. Quṭb, *Social Justice in Islam*, 183.
2. Madelung, *The Succession to Muḥammad*, 140.
3. Ibid, 197-8.

Madelung then analyzes the role of cursing within Muʿāwiya's political finesse. ʿAlī is portrayed by Muʿāwiya as a sworn enemy, in a manner which differs from the works of contemporary scholars, with the animosity displayed in public arenas:

> Particularly useful for Muʿāwiya's purposes was the public cursing of ʿAlī in Kūfah where, he hoped, it would bring out into the open the latent opposition to Umayyad rule, thus facilitating his measures of repression.[1]

1. Madelung, *The Succession to Muḥammad*, 335.

Muʿāwiya's Treatment of Rebellions

Muʿāwiya had cleverly chosen al-Mughīrah b. Shuʿbah al-Thaqafī, a man of experience, as governor of Kūfah.[1] Al-Mughīrah could now help control any emerging political rivals for Muʿāwiya in Kūfah and, indeed, dissenters. As soon as he came into power, al-Mughīrah would have to end the revolt of Muʿayn b. ʿAbdullāh al-Muḥāribī and ensured that he was executed. Abū Laylā, ally of Banī al-Ḥārith b. Kaʿb was also killed. He had shouted, *'Taḥkīm!'* (arbitration), in the mosque and wanted to revolt in Kūfah. Maʿqil b. Qays al-Riyāḥī was appointed by al-Mughīrah to kill him in the Sawād.

Muʿāwiya had appointed al-Mughīrah in Kūfah and ʿAbdullāh b. ʿĀmīr in Baṣra. ʿAbdullāh had to face the Khawārij but was seemingly lenient with them. ʿIbādah b. Qurṣ al-Laythī, known as a companion of Muḥammad, was killed by a group of the Khawārij who had been led by Sahm b. Ghālib al-Hujaymī. They killed him as well as his wife and son. ʿAbdullāh caught them, but did not kill them, and ensured that they were to be granted amnesty. He therefore went against an order from Muʿāwiya to execute them.[2] Muʿāwiya dismissed him because:

---

1. Al-Balādhurī, *Ansāb al-Ashrāf*, vol. 4A, 139-40.

2. Ibn al-Athīr, vol. 3, 417-418.

> He had some difficulties in his dealings with the the tribesmen in Baṣra itself. This was because large numbers of new immigrants coming into Baṣra had caused some tension between the different tribal groups. Muʿāwiya, who was alarmed by the situation, removed Ibn ʿĀmīr in 44/664, replacing him with the redoubtable Zīyād b. Abihī.[1]

These two appointments were signs of the *ḥilm* of Muʿāwiya. He knew who to appoint and when to replace them and with whom to replace them. Al-Mughīrah was protecting Kūfah for him and Zīyād was now ensuring the smooth running of affairs in Baṣra. Al-Mughīrah was constantly aware of the plans of the Khawārij. Men such as Muʿadh b. Juwayn al-Ṭa'ī, al-Mustawrid b. ʿUllafa al-Taymī and Ḥayyān b. Dhabyan al-Sulamī were seeking to make a breakthrough in Kūfah, especially Ḥayyān, who had been in al-Rayy since 38/658. The meetings were held in the house of Ḥayyān and were attended by twenty of the Khawārij. Qabīḍa b. al-Dāmūn was appointed to break the meeting, capture and imprison the leaders in the prisons of Kūfah. These people had felt oppressed and at the same time felt Islamic law was not being implemeneted. However, al-Mustawrid escaped and al-Mughīrah met each and every tribal leader to ensure that they kept an eye out for the rebels, and if they did not, or if a rebel was from their tribe, then the whole tribe would be imprisoned. This form of governance had not been witnessed in the reigns of any of the first caliphs.[2]

Furthermore, Mughīrah would ensure that any of the enemies of the central government would fight each other. Qabīḍa b. al-Dāmūn was ordered to ensure three thousand of the Shīʿīs of Kūfah would be sent under Maʿqil b. Qays al-Riyāḥī, a Shīʿī, to fight al-Mustawrid.

---

1. Shaban, *Islamic History*, 85-86.

2. Al-Ṭabarī, *Tārīkh*, vol. 2, 32-33.

Both died at al-Madhār, a Khārijite and a Shī'ī fighting each other with al-Mughīrah instigating the war. Indeed, anyone whose loyalty was in question would not be given any sanctuary, including Shabīb b. Bajra al-Ashja'ī who had fought against 'Alī at al-Nahrawān was killed by Khālid b. 'Urfuṭa in 'Unquf near Kūfah.[1]

Zīyād b. Abīhī made a unanimous announcement when appointed as the governor (45/664) of Baṣra which embodied the message of the government.

> I swear I will never be remiss in punishing the client for the Sire, the father for the son, the healthy for the sick, the staying for the fugitive, the obedient for the unruly, until the man on meeting will say, 'Save yourself Sa'd for Sa'īd has perished'.[2]

Those who were pardoned or given amnesty would no longer receive such treatment under Zīyād. As an example, Sahm was killed and Zīyād b. Mālik al-Bāhilī was to be placed under house arrest in Baṣra under the watchful eye of Muslim b. 'Amr al-Bāhilī. On the night that Zīyād asked to see Zīyād b. Mālik he was not there. This led to his execution and his body was not even given a burial but thrown towards a resident tribe.[3] Zīyād was ruthless but the act of throwing a body with no burial was unprecedented.[4] Furthermore, when 'Abbad b. Ḥusayn al-Ṭā'ī led a revolt in Baṣra, he was mercilessly caught and executed by Bishr b. 'Utbah al-Tamīmī under the orders of Zīyād. The latter would eventually take charge of both Kūfah and Baṣra when al-Mughīrah died in 50/670. One governor would administer both districts for the first time. He would ensure

1. Al-Balādhurī, *Ansāb al-Ashrāf*, vol. 4A, 141.
2. Al-Ṭabarī, *Tārīkh*, vol. 2, 74.
3. Al-Balādhurī, *Ansāb al-Ashrāf*, vol. 4A, 148-49.
4. Ibid149.

that he spent six months in Baṣra and six months in Kūfah.

His strength as governor would be revealed through the revolts that would be led when he was not present. An increase in revolts began because of his strictness with his fiscal policies and the purging of records which included the names of the deceased of the Khawārij. Corruption would then be limited and people would not abuse the system.[1] When he left Baṣra, he would announce Samar b. Jundab al-Fazārī as his successor and some Khawārij would seek to revolt including the likes of Qurayb b. Murra al-ʿAzdī and Zaḥāf b. Zahr al-Ṭāʾī. They had the audacity to march through the streets and kill. When Zīyād returned he unleashed a warning that if the people of Baṣra did not cooperate with him then they would feel the force of his administration and rule. Their annual stipends would also be cut off.[2] This announcement led to the heads of the tribes of ʿAlī and Rāsib to besiege the Banī Yashkur and kill Qurayb and his companions. If your tribe was made up of a Kharijite, people would ensure that the person would be taken to Zīyād.[3]

Zīyād was equally ruthless with the women of the community. In an unprecedented move, he declared that even the women of the Khawārij would be killed if they were known to be plotting against the state. Questions are raised about Muʿāwiya's silence on this issue as this was not known to be a practice of Prophet Muḥammad. Women were to be hung naked if they were following the ideologies of Qurayb and Zaḥāf. Jārīyah, a women of the Khārijites decided that she had to speak out against Zīyād and his policies. She was to be executed and hung as a message to all Baṣran women who supported the Khawārij. The caliph was silent when advice and guidance was

1. Shaban, *Islamic History*, 87.

2. Al-Balādhurī, *Ansāb al-Ashrāf*, vol. 4A, 150-152.

3. Al-Mubarrad, *al-Kāmil*, vol. 3, 245.

necessary to stop the ruthless Zīyād.[1] By the end of his rule, none of the Khārijites could rebel against him, male or female. Hence one may argue this was the reason Mu'āwiya was silent. Zīyād's message was continued by his son 'Ubaydullāh, who would cut off the feet of 'Urwah b. 'Adīyah b. Ḥandhala al-Tamīmī when he had the bravery to criticise his father's policies. He also had to foil the revolt of Ṭawwaf b. Ghallāq. When 'Urwah's brother Abū Bilāl sought to revolt in Darabjerd, he was killed by Ibn Zīyād's commander 'Abbād b. 'Alqama b. 'Amr al-Mazinī al-Tamīmī in 61/681.[2]

1. Al-Balādhurī, *Ansāb al-Ashrāf*, vol. 4A, 152-153.

2. Al-Balādhurī, *Ansāb al-Ashrāf*, vol. 4A, 159.

The Execution of Ḥujr b. ʿAdī

Muʿāwiya did not face the animosity from the partisans of ʿAlī as he had faced from the Khawārij. In the first ten years of his rule, there was relative peace between the two factions. ʿAbdullāh b. Amīr, the governor of Baṣra, and al-Mughīrah b. Shuʿbah would employ prominent Shīʿī such as Sharik b. al-Aʿwar al-Ḥārithī to fight the Khawārīj. However, where Muʿāwiya's *ḥilm* is to be questioned is making permissible the cursing of ʿAlī on the pulpits.

This was an act unprecedented in Islamic history and would result in uproar from the followers of ʿAlī. His followers would constantly display their loyalty towards their leader by narrating his merits. Saʿsaʿah b. Sahwān al-ʿAbdī was once informed by al-Mughīrah when hearing that he would narrate the merits of ʿAlī publically that –

I warn you to stop doing so, and to remember that you will not say a thing in praise of ʿAlī which I do not know. If you want to do so, you can do it among your kinsmen in your houses and in secret but in the mosque I shall not permit it and the caliph himself will not tolerate this or forgive me for this if I allow you to do it.[1]

Surprisingly enough, the statement that the merits of ʿAlī would not be tolerated in the mosque, but the cursing of ʿAlī had become an institution, were approved by the caliph and the governor.

1. Al-Ṭabarī, citing Abū Mikhnāf, *Tarikh*, vol. 2, 38.

After the year of the community (*ʿam al-jamāʿa*), Muʿāwiya wrote a letter to his tax collectors in which he said, 'Let the conquered people refrain from mentioning any merit to Abū Turāb or his kinsmen'. So in every village and on every pulpit preachers stood up cursing ʿAlī, disowning him, disparaging him and his house. In another letter he wrote, 'Make search for those you can find who were partisans of ʿUthmān and those who supported his rule and those who uphold his merits and qualities. Seek their company, gain access to them and honor them. Write down for me what everybody relates, as well as his name, that of his father and clan'.

Thus, they did until they had increased the number of merits and qualities of ʿUthmān. In exchange he sent them presents, garments, gifts and [documents of] pieces of land. This was showered over Arabs *mawali* alike and it occurred on a large scale in every city, the people competing in ranks and worldly honors. Every lowly individual who went to any governors of Muʿāwiya and related about ʿUthmān a merit or a virtue was received kindly, his name was taken down and he was given preferential treatment.

Regular public cursing of ʿAlī, identified as the soul of the Prophet, in the congregational prayers thus remained a vital institution, which was not abolished until sixty years later by ʿUmar II (ʿUmar b. ʿAbd al-ʿAzīz). Marwān clearly recognized the importance of the cursing as a tool of government. He told ʿAlī b. al-Ḥusayn, 'No one was more temperate (*akaff*) towards our master than your master'. ʿAlī b. al-Ḥusayn asked him, 'Why do you curse him then from the pulpits?' He answered, 'Our reign would not be sound without that'. (*Lā yastaqīmu lana hadha illa bi hadha*).

Particularly useful for Muʿāwiya's purposes was the public cursing of ʿAlī in Kūfah where, he hoped, it would bring out into the open the latent opposition to Umayyad rule, thus facilitating his measures of repression. When he appointed al-Mughīra b. Shuʿba governor of

Kūfah, he instructed him, 'Never desist from abusing and censuring 'Alī, from praying for God's mercy and forgiveness for 'Uthmān, from disgracing the followers of 'Alī, from removing them and refusing to listen to them. Moreover, never cease praising the partisans of 'Uthmān, bringing them close to you, and listening to them'.

The Shī'ī of 'Alī would not accept what they viewed as an act of injustice against the tenants of Islam. 'Alī was a caliph, son-in-law of Muḥammad and a nobleman of great pedigree. Unlike the Khawārij, the Shī'ī who stood up and revolted were men of great history and virtue, amongst them Ḥujr b. 'Adī. Al-Mughīrah had cursed 'Alī in his sermon. This caused outrage with Ḥujr and other worshippers standing who raised a cry that they would not accept such words and policies from the government. Al-Dīnawarī narrates that al-Mughīrah tried to win Ḥujr's support with a sum of five thousand dirhams, but this seems unlikely as the diwān was providing Ḥujr with 2,500 dirhams at the time.[1] Al-Mughīrah died in 50/670 and Zīyād became governor of both Kūfah and Baṣra.

Ḥujr and Zīyād had known each other through previous skirmishes, both on the side of 'Alī and when they fought in opposition. Ḥujr was offered sums of money and different ranks within the government hierarchy but refused all the advances made by Zīyād.[2] 'Amr b. Ḥurayth al-Makhzūmī had been appointed as Zīyād's representative in Kūfah when he had left for Baṣra. 'Amr's speech, anti-'Alī in its stance, was interrupted by Ḥujr and his partisans. Sinān b. Ḥurayth al-Ḍabbī was sent to inform Zīyād in Kūfah of what had happened. He conveyed to him the message that Ḥujr and his followers were now in a position of strength in Kūfah.

1. Al-Dinawarī, *Al-Akhbār al-Ṭiwāl*, 223; Ibn al-Athīr, *Usad al-Ghaba*, vol. 1, 386.

2. Al-Isfahānī, *Kitāb al-Aghānī* (Beirut, 1970), vol. 3, 16.

Zīyād sent warnings to Ḥujr through personalities such as Jarīr b. ʿAbdullāh al-Bajālī and Khālid b. ʿUrfuta al-ʿUdhrī that such behavior would not be tolerated. Ḥujr could not tolerate their public attacks seeking to defile the character of ʿAlī, which he believed to be attacks against the very core of the religion of Islam. Shaddād b. al-Haytham al-Hilālī was sent to Ḥujr but he did not make any breakthrough. Zīyād was outraged and conveyed his outrage to the chiefs of Kūfah including Qays b. al-Walīd b. ʿAbd Shams b. al-Mughīrah and Abū Burḍa b. Abū Mūsa al-Ashʿarī. He said:

> O people of Kūfah, you are wounding with one hand and sympathizing with the other. Your bodies are with me but your hearts are with Ḥujr that fool. You are with me while your kinsmen are with Ḥujr. This is dishonesty. You have to show me unqualified loyalty otherwise I shall send against you people who will bring you back and will destroy your pride.

The chiefs of Kūfah vowed that their kinsmen would support Zīyād and leave Ḥujr.[1] Interesting to note the language used by Zīyād in describing Ḥujr as a fool and that the people of Kūfah were either with him or against him. The people of Kūfah's support for Ḥujr indicates distrust, or, indeed, disenchantment with Zīyād's rule, and a question mark on Muʿāwiya's choice of one governor for two districts.

Zīyād, recognizing the power of Ḥujr's stand, sent out groups to find Ḥujr. Muḥammad b. al-Ashʿath b. Qays was given three days to find Ḥujr. If he did not, then all the plam trees that he owned and his houses would be destroyed and he would be executed. Ḥujr had to flee, including movements made from al-Nakhaʿī, an area led by ʿAbdullāh b. al-Ḥārith al-Nakhaʿī towards ʿAzd. Muḥammad received

1. Al-Baladhurī, *Ansāb al-Ashrāf*, vol.4A, 214-215.

a letter from Ḥujr that he would surrender himself if he were to be pardoned and sent to Muʿāwiya, in expectation of amnesty from the caliph. Ḥujr b. Yazīd al-Kindī and Jarīr b. ʿAbdullāh al-Bajālī accompanied Muḥammad to Zīyād who granted Ḥujr amnesty in a prison cell for ten days.[1] Thirteen of Ḥujr's loyal partisans were pursued and captured by Zīyād. Saʿd b. Nimrān al-Hamdhānī, ʿUtbah b. al-Akhnās al-Saʿdī, ʿAbdul Raḥman b. Ḥasanal-Anzī, ʿAbdullāh b. Ḥawīyyah al-Tamīmī, Kidam b. Ḥayyān al-ʿAnsī, Warqaʿ b. Sumayyah al-Bajālī, ʿAṣīm b. ʿAwf al-Bajālī, Qabīṣa b. Dubaya b. Ḥarmala al-ʿAbsī, Qabīṣa b. Dubaya, Sayfi b. Faṣil al-Shaybānī, Sharik b. Shaddad al-Ḥadrāmī and al-Arqām b. ʿAbdullāh al-Kindī.[2] Amongst them was ʿAmr b. Ḥumq al-Khuzāʿī, a companion of Muḥammad. Reports indicate he escaped but was caught by ʿAbdul-Raḥman b. ʿAbdullāh b. ʿUthmān al-Thaqafī, the governor of Mosul, was killed and paraded around.[3]

When Ḥujr and his companions rebelled, Zīyād attacked their stance and revolt. He first forged a story that they were looking to dissolve the caliphate of Muʿāwiya by revolting against his governor in Iraq. Secondly, he used their love for the family of the Prophet (the Ahl al-Bayt) as a negative belief which had to be destroyed.[4] The origin of Islam was built on the foundation of love and its expression for Muḥammad's near ones, but was now seen as a threatening armour in the hands of Ḥujr and his followers. Seventy men of different tribes signed the accusations of Zīyād.[5]

Waʾil b. Ḥujr al-Ḥadrāmī and Kathīr b. Shihāb al-Ḥarithī were ordered to ensure Ḥujr was taken to Muʿāwiya, who refused to meet

1. Al-Ṭabarī, *Tārīkh*, vol. 2, 121.

2. Al-Baladhurī, *Ansāb al-Ashrāf*, vol. 4A, 218-219.

3. Al-Ṭabarī, *Tārīkh*, vol. 2, 136.

4. Al-Baldhurī, *Ansāb al-Ashrāf*, Vol.4A, 236-237.

5. Ibid, 223.

him, although he did meet Zīyād's messengers. Two miles from Damascus in Marj ʿAdhra, Ḥujr and his companions were imprisoned.[1] Yazīd b. Asad al-Bajālī sought to advise Muʿāwiya to spread Ḥujr and his followers to different parts of the region and thus break their stand against him. Zīyād however wanted a quick resolution to end their lives and keep stability in the region. 'If you desire the stability of this *miṣr*, please do not send Ḥujr and his followers to Kūfah again'.[2]

Each of Ḥujr's followers had kinsmen in Syria who sought to mediate on their tribesmen's behalf. ʿAsim and Warqa, both Bajalis were represented by Jarīr b. ʿAbdullah al–Bajalī. Saʿd b. Numrān al-Hamdhanī received the backing of Humrah b. Mālik al-Hamdhānī, Karīm b. ʿAfīf al-Kathʿamī received the backing of Shamir b. ʿAbdullāh al-Khathʿāmī. Ḥujr was represented by Mālik b. Ḥubayra al-Sakūnī, but to no avail. Muʿāwiya firmly belived that Ḥujr was the instigator and ordered that this innocent man who stood up against the injustice of the pulpits of Kūfah was to be executed alongside six of his followers.[3] Shaban states that for Muʿāwiya 'it was effective, but unusually rash and high handed'.[4]

The policemen took Ḥujr and his faithful companions to Marj ʿAdhra', where they were quickly imprisoned. Muʿāwiya and Zīyād then exchanged letters with each other. Not only did they bring Muʿāwiya's order to kill Ḥujr and his companions, they also brought shrouds with them. 'Indeed the Commander of the Faithful has ordered me to kill you, for you are the root of error, the origin of unbelief and tyranny, and the supporter of Abū Turāb. He has ordered me to kill your companions unless you retract your unbelief, curse

1. Al-Ṭabarī, *Tārīkh*, vol. 2, 134.
2. Al-Baladhurī, *Ansāb al-Ashrāf*, vol.4A, 223.
3. Al-Baladhurī, *Ansāb al-Ashrāf*, vol.4A, 224; al-Yaʿqūbī, *Tārīkh*, vol. 2, 231.
4. Shaban, *Islamic History*, 89-90.

your leader and renounce him', Muʿāwiya's officials declared to Ḥujr. 'Indeed patience towards the punishment of the sword is easier for us than what you summon us to. Meeting Allāh, His Apostle, and his *waṣī* (Imam ʿAlī) is more attractive to us than entering the fire', said Ḥujr and his companions.

The graves were dug for Ḥujr and his companions. They performed their prayers throughout the night. When morning came, the policemen went to retrieve them. 'Let me perform the ritual ablution and say my prayers', requested Ḥujr. They let him pray, and after he was finished they took him away. 'By Allāh, I had not performed a prayer lighter than this prayer', he said. 'Were it not for that, you think that I am impatient of death, I would increase it'.

Then Ḥujr said: 'O Allāh, we ask you to show enmity towards our people. Indeed, the Kūfans have testified against us, and the Syrians have come to kill us. By Allāh, If you kill me in the village of ʿAdhra', I will be the first Muslim horseman to be killed in its valley, and the first Muslim man at whom its dogs will bark'.[1]

Then Hudba b. Fayyad al-Qudaʿī walked towards him with his sword while Ḥujr had his. Hudba trembled and said to Ḥujr: 'You have claimed that you are patient towards death. Therefore renounce your leader and we will let you go'.

Ḥujr replied: 'Of course, I am patient towards death. For I see a grave has been dug, a shroud has been spread, and a sword has been drawn. Indeed, by Allāh, even if I am impatient towards death, I will not say what displeases the Lord!'

1. Ibn al-Athīr, *al-Kāmil fī Taʿrikh,* vol. 3, 192. Ibn Saʿd and Musʿab al-Zubarī have narrated the following on the authority of al-Ḥākim, who said: 'He was killed at Marj ʿAdhra' according to Muʿāwiya's orders. It was Ḥujr who conquered it (Marj ʿAdhra'), then he was killed at it'. This is the meaning of Ḥujr's words: "...and the first Muslim man at whom its dogs will bark". He meant the day when he conquered it'.

A few close associates of Muʿāwiya interceded for seven companions of Ḥujr. The rest of Ḥujr's companions were put to the sword. Ḥujr's final words were, 'Leave me shackled with iron and stained with blood. For I will meet Muʿāwiya on the straight path tomorrow. I will testify against him before Allāh'. Muʿāwiya mentioned these words of Ḥujr when he was about to die: 'Ḥujr, my day will be long because of you', he said.

Muʿāwiya performed the hajj after he had killed Ḥujr; he happened to pass by the house of ʿAʾisha. He asked permission to enter her home, and she permitted him inside. When he sat down, she said to him: 'Did you not fear Allāh when you killed Ḥujr and his companions?'[1] Then she added: 'Were it not for the critical situation, we would not have let Ḥujr be killed. By Allāh, he performed the greater and the lesser hajj'.[2]

Shurayh b. Hānī had wrote to Muʿāwiya concerning Ḥujr and had given him a religious opinion in which he said that it was forbidden for Muʿāwiya to shed the blood of Ḥujr and to take his possessions. Shurayh had said about Ḥujr, 'He was among those who performed the ritual prayers, paid zakat, frequently performed the lesser and the greater hajj, enjoined (the people) to do good deeds and prevented them from doing evil deeds. It was forbidden to shed his blood and to take his property'.[3]

Ibn ʿUmar began asking the people about Ḥujr from the day he was captured. While Ibn ʿUmar was walking in the market, he was told that Ḥujr had been killed. He burst into tears and left.[4]

ʿAbd al-Raḥmān b. al-Ḥārith b. Hishām came to Muʿāwiya, after

1. Al-Ṭabarī, *Taʾrikh*, vol. 6, 156.
2. Ibn al-Athīr, *al-Kāmil fi al-Taʾrikh*, vol. 3, 193.
3. Al-Ṭabarī, *Taʾrikh*, vol. 6, 153.
4. Ibid.

the latter had killed Ḥujr, and said to him: 'When did the clemency of Abū Sūfyān leave you?' Muʿāwiya replied: 'It left me when those who were like you in clemency left me. Ibn Sumayya (Zīyād b. Abīh) provoked me, so I carried that out'. Then ʿAbd al-Raḥmān said: 'By Allāh, the Arabs will never regard you as the one who has clemency and a [good] opinion. You killed the people whom the prisoners from the Muslims sent to you'.

Many people from Kinda, al-Sikūn, and Yemen supported Malik b. Hubayra al-Sikūnī. So Malik was able to freely say to Muʿāwiya the following words when he refused to release Ḥujr from prison: 'By Allāh, we are in no need of Muʿāwiya more than Muʿāwiya is in no need of us. We have alternates among his peoples, while he has no successor from us among the people'.[1]

Al-Ḥasan al-Baṣrī said: 'Muʿāwiya had four flaws. Firstly, his appointment of troublemakers for this community so that he stole its rule without consultation with its members, while there was a remnant of the companions and possessors of virtue among them. Secondly, his appointment of his son as his successor after him, a drunkard and a habitual drinker of alcohol who wears silk and plays *tunbur*. Thirdly, he claimed Zīyād [as his own child] while the Apostle of Allāh, may Allāh bless him and his family, said, "The baby is to the bed (son of *zina*, or adultery) and the prostitute is stoned". Fourthly, the execution of Ḥujr. Woe unto him from Ḥujr and his companions'.[2]

After Muʿāwiya had murdered these noble Muslims, and after he had performed his hajj, he met al-Ḥusayn b. ʿAlī, peace be upon him, in Mecca and said to him proudly: 'Have you heard what we have

1. See also: Ibn ʿAbd al-Birr al-Malikī, *al-Istiʿāb*. Ibn al-ʿAthīr, *Asad al-Ghāba fi Tamyīz al-Ṣaḥāba*. ʿAlī Khān, *al-Darajāt al-Rāfiʿa*. Al-Shaykh al-Ṭūsī, *al-Amālī*.

2. Ibn Kathīr, *al-Bidāyah wa al-Nihāyah* (Beirut: Maktabah al Ma'ārif, 1966), vol. 8, 130-140.

done to Ḥujr, his companions, and his Shiʿa (followers) who were the Shiʿa of your father?' Al-Ḥusayn asked: 'What have you done to them?' Muʿāwiya replied: 'We have killed them, shrouded them, prayed over them, and buried them'. Al-Ḥusayn, peace be upon him, smiled, and then he said: 'Muʿāwiya, the people will bring suit against you (before Allāh). If we killed your followers, we would not shroud them, nor would we pray over them, nor would we bury them'.[1]

Among the companions who were killed with Ḥujr were Shurayk b. Shaddād, Thaddād al-Haḍramī, and Ṣayfī b. Fasīl al-Shaybānī. The latter was one of the best companions of Ḥujr. It is said that he had an iron heart, strong belief in God, and polite speech. He was captured with Ḥujr and brought before Zīyād. 'O enemy of Allāh, what do you think of Abū Turāb (i.e., Imam ʿAlī)?,' he said to him. 'I do not know anyone named Abū Turāb', replied Ṣayfī. 'You know him very well', Zīyād continued. 'I don't know him', answered Ṣayfī. 'Do you not know ʿAlī b. Abū Ṭālib?' asked Zīyād. 'Yes', answered Ṣayfī. To which Zīyād replied incredulously, '*That* is Abū Turāb!'. 'No, that is Abū al-Ḥasan and al-Ḥusayn', said Ṣayfī. So Zīyād's police chief said to Ṣayfī: 'The Emīr said to you: "He is Abū Turāb", and you say: "No". Do you want me to tell lies as the Emīr does? Do you want me to falsely testify?' asked Ṣayfī. 'Bring me the rod', said Zīyād. When the rod was brought to Zīyād, he said to Ṣayfī: 'What do you say now?' 'These are the best words which I have said concerning a servant from the believing servants of Allāh', replied Ṣayfī. 'Hit his shoulder with the rod till he sticks to the ground', said Zīyād. So Ṣayfī was hit a number of times until his body stuck to the ground.

1. Al-Majlisī, *Bihar al-Anwar*. Al-Ṭabarī has narrated a tradition similar to this one on the authority of al-Ḥasan. That is incorrect for the tragedy of Ḥujr and his companions happened two years after the death of al-Ḥasan. A similar tradition has been narrated by Ibn al-ʿAthīr on the authority of al-Ḥasan al-Baṣrī who said: 'By the Lord of the Kaʿaba, they have instituted a proof against them'.

Then Zīyād requested that the police stop beating Ṣayfī. 'What do you think of ʿAlī now?,' Zīyād asked. 'By Allāh, even if you cut me to pieces with razors and knifes, I will not say except what you have heard from me', answered Ṣayfī. 'You should curse him otherwise I will cut off your neck', said Zīyād. 'Then cut it off', he replied. 'Push him in the neck. Tie him up with the shackles, and throw him into prison', shouted Zīyād. Thus Ṣayfī joined the caravan of death with Ḥujr, and was among those blessed people who died as martyrs at the Marj of ʿAdhra'.

Then there was ʿAbd al-Raḥmān b. Ḥasan al-ʿAnzī. He was sent to prison along with Ḥujr while he was shackled. When he arrived at the Marj of ʿAdhra', he asked the police to send him to Muʿāwiya because he thought that Muʿāwiya would be kinder to him than Ibn Zīyād. When he came to Muʿāwiya, the latter said to him: 'Brother of Rābī'a, what do you have to say about ʿAlī ?' 'Leave me and do not ask me (about him), for that is better for you', replied ʿAbd al-Raḥmān. 'By Allāh, I will not leave you alone until you answer', said Muʿāwiya.

ʿAbd al-Raḥmān said: 'I testify that he was among those who remembered Allāh very much, enjoined the truth, undertook justice, and forgave the people'. 'What do you say concerning ʿUthmān?' asked Muʿāwiya. 'He was the first to open the door of injustice and to close the door of truth', answered ʿAbd al-Raḥmān. 'You have killed yourself', said Muʿāwiya. 'Rather, you have killed yourself', said ʿAbd al-Raḥmān. Then Muʿāwiya returned him to Zīyād in Kūfah and promptly ordered him to kill him in a malevolent manner.

'On the day when the policemen of Muʿāwiya imprisoned him along with his companions at the Marj of ʿAdhra' ʿAbd al-Raḥmān said the following words: 'O Allāh, make me among those whom You honor through their [the Umayyads'] disgrace, and be pleased with me. I subjected myself to the possibilty of being murdered many times, but Allāh refused (that) except what He willed'.

In his book *Tarikh al-Kūfah* , Ḥabbata al-ʿAranī has mentioned ʿAbd al-Raḥmān as follows: "Abd al-Raḥmān b. Ḥassan al-ʿAnzī was among the companions of ʿAlī, peace be upon him. He lived in Kūfah and used to provoke the people against the Banū Umayya. So Zīyād captured him and sent him to Sham. Muʿāwiya summoned him to renounce ʿAlī, peace be upon him, but ʿAbd al-Raḥmān answered Muʿāwiya rudely. So Muʿāwiya returned him to Zīyād, and Zīyād killed him'. Ibn al-ʿAthīr[1] and al-Ṭabarī[2] narrate that Zīyād buried ʿAbd al-Raḥmān alive at the Qis of al-Natif.[3]

Also among the companions who died with Ḥujr was Qubayṣa b. Rabīʿa al-ʿAbasī, although he was called Qubayṣa b. Dubayʿa by some historians. Qubayṣa was a brave man who decided to resist the corrupt Umayyads along with his community. The commander of the police gave him his oath that his blood would not be shed and his property would not be taken, and he put his hand in their hands according to the covenant of security and protection which the Arabs followed before and after Islam. But it seems that the Umayyads abandoned the morals of the Arabs and Muslims, or that they simply understood that such morals were a mere means for victory and violence. So (Qubayṣa) b. Dubayʿa al-ʿAbasī was brought before Zīyād, who said to him: 'By Allāh, I will do (something) for you to distract you from creating discord and revolting against the governors'. Qubayṣa said: 'I have come to you according to the security covenant'. 'Take him to prison', said Zīyād.

Qubayṣa was among the people who were shackled and taken to their deaths because of patience. Before the policemen took Ḥujr and his companions prisoner, they had passed by Qubayṣa's house. Qubayṣa saw his daughters looking at him and weeping. So he said

1. Ibn al-ʿAthir, *al-Kamil fi al-Taʿrikh*, vol. 3, 192.

2. Al-Ṭabarī, *Taʿrikh*, vol. 6, 155.

3. The eastern bank of the Euphrates.

to Wāʿil and Kathīr, the two policemen taking him to jail: 'Allow me to see my family'. When he approached his weeping daughters, he kept silent for an hour, and then he said to them: 'Be silent'. So they remained silent. Then he said to them: 'Fear Allāh, the Great and Almighty. Be patient. Indeed I hope that Allāh, my Lord, will grant me one of the two good things during this challenge of mine - either martyrdom or returning to you. It is Allāh, the Most High, Who gives You your provisions. He is Living, and never dies. I hope that He will not leave you. I hope that He will protect me so that I can return to you'. Then Qubayṣa was taken away. The hopeless family spent the night weeping and praying, just as Muʿāwiya had wanted. There were many daughters similar to Dubayʿa's who had suffered such tragedies.

Al-Ṭabarī said: 'Qubayṣa b. Dubayʿa fell into the hands of Abū Sharīf al-Baddī. So Qubayṣa said to him: "Indeed there is bad blood between my people and your people. So let someone other than you kill me". Abū Sharīf said: "Kinship is obedient to your wishes". Then al-Quḍāʿī killed Qubayṣa'.[1]

Also among the fallen were Kaddam b. Hayyān al-ʿAnzī and Muhriz b. Shahāb b. Būjayr b. Sufyān b. Khālid b. Munqir al-Tamīmī. The latter was among the chiefs of the people, and from among the loyal and pious Shīʿites who were known for their devotion to the Ahlulbayt. Muhriz was the commander of the left wing of the army headed by Maʿqāl b. Qays, who had waged war against the Khāijites in the year 43 AH. During those three battles, the army of Maʿqāl numbered three thousand people from among the loyal Shīʿites and their horsemen, as al-Tabari described in his book.[2]

1. Al-Ṭabarī, *Ta'rikh*, vol. 6, 156.

2. Al-Ṭabarī, *Ta'rikh*, vol. 6, 108.

Analysis of the Incident

What Khaled Keshk does not take into account amongst others who seek to defend Muʿāwiya is the pre-Islamic definition of *ḥilm* and its usage. In the pre-Islamic definition of *ḥilm*, the *ḥalīm* was a person renowned for his:

> calmness, balanced mind, self-control and steadiness of judgement. A ḥalīm is a man who knows how to smother his feelings, to overcome his own blind passions and to remain tranquil and undisturbed whatever happens to him, however much he may be provoked.[1]

The *jāhil* was a:

> hot-blooded impetuous man, who tends to lose his self-control on the slightest provocation, and consequently to act wrecklessly, driven by an uncontrollable blind passion, without reflecting on the disastrous consequence this behavior might lead to. It is the behavior pattern peculiar to a man of an extremely touch and passionate nature, who has no control

1. Izutsu, *God and Man in the Koran: Semantics of the Koranic Weltanschauung* (Tokyo: The Keio Institute of Cultural and Linguistic Studies, 1964), 205.

> of his own feelings and emotions, and who therefore, easily surrenders himself to the dictates of violent passions, losing the sense of what is right and what is wrong.[1]

Muʿāwiya' s act of killing Ḥujr was more an act of *jahl* than *ḥilm* for it can be seen as an act of hot bloodedness as well as wrecklessness, with very little display of tranquility and calmness when these attributes were requires.

Keshk furthermore seeks to convey the theory that there is not a need for the historians to emphasize on certain elements of the story of Ḥujr, and that when this is done, they are taking away from the fact that 'these sources had a primary purpose that was lost on modern scholars in their use of the Ḥujr story'.[2] The reply however is that the emphasis on these elements was to portray a clearer understanding of the motives and the backgrounds of the execution. The historians are all in agreement on four major parts of the narrative. The first is a discussion of the disagreement which occurred between Ḥujr, al-Mughīrah and Zīyād. The second is that they discuss the background to his disaobedience of the authorities in Kūfah, the third is his arrest and the fourth is his execution. Keshk states that while they all agree they tend to emphasize one incident over another. Emphasis of one incident above another does not hide the over-arching question mark as to whether Muʿāwiyas conclusive decision concerning Ḥujr was that of a *ḥalīm* or that of a *jāhil*.

A study of the works of the historians displays how their conclusions are that Muʿāwiya was the man who made the decision to kill Ḥujr. While Khalīf b. Khayyaṭ does not elaborate further on the

1. Ibid.

2. Keshk, K. *The Historians Muʿāwiya; The Depiction of Muʿāwiya in the Early Islamic Sources* (Germany: Vdm Verlag Dr. MullerAktienGesellschaft, 2008), 104.

background of the incident and simply states that Mu'āwiya killed Ḥujr in the year 50 AH,[1] Ibn A'tham clearly discusses that there was an active killing spree taking place at the time against the supporters of 'Alī by Zīyād, which was undertaken to please Mu'āwiya. This does not reflect well on Mu'āwiya's *ḥilm* as here he is portrayed as the bloodthirsty despot of the *jāhil* age.[2]

Furthermore, al-Balādhurī[3] using Rawḥ b. 'Abd al-Mu'min and 'Umar b. Shabba b. 'Abida b. Zayd b. Raiṭ al-Numayrī, al-Ṭabarī from 'Alī b. Ḥasan and Muslim b. Abī Muslim al-Ḥaramī[4] and Ibn 'Asākīr[5] using Hishām b. Ḥasan concentrate on portraying two very important themes in the incident. The first theme which they are unanimous on is Ḥujr is a martyr and not a rebel or a dissident figure. Secondly, Ḥujr is the man of piety and not Mu'āwiya or his soldiers. Mu'āwiya's lack of self control is displayed by the fact that historians are unanimous that it was Mu'āwiya who would encourage his governors to curse 'Alī publically. This begun under the leadership of al-Mughīrah and continued in the reign of Zīyād. Keshk does not seek to accept that all the early historians are in agreement that it was Mu'āwiya who would find pleasure in the public cursing of 'Alī. This important prelude to the incident of the killing of Ḥujr is narrated

1. Khalīfah b. Khayyaṭ, Abū 'Amr. *Tārīkh Khalīfah b. Khayyaṭ*, ed. Muṣṭafa Najib Fawaz and Ḥikmat Fawwāz (Beirut, Dar al-Kutub al-'Ilmiyyah, 1995), 131.

2. Al-Kūfī, Ibn A'tham. *Kitāb al-Fūtūḥ*, 8 vols. (Ḥaydarabād: Da'irat al-ma'ārif al-Uthmaniyyah, 1968-75), 203.

3. Al-Balādhurī, Aḥmad b. Yaḥyā b. Jabīr. *Ansāb al-ashrāf*, vol 4/1, ed. Iḥsān 'Abbās (Wiesbaden: Franz Steiner, 1979), vol. 4, 243.

4. Al-Ṭabarī, Muḥammad b. Jarīr, *Tārīkh al rusūl wa-al-mulūk*, ed. Muḥammad Abū al-Faḍl Ibrahīm, 11 vols. (Cairo: Dar al-Ma'ārif, 1960-1970), vol. 5, 256.

5. Ibn 'Asākir, 'Alī b. al-Ḥasan. *Tārīkh Medinat Dimashq*, ed. Muḥibb al-Dīn Abū Sa'īd 'Umar b. Gharama al-'Amrāwī, 70 vols. (Beirut: Dar al-Fikr, 1995-1998).

by al-Balādhurī,[1] al-Yaʿqūbī, al-Ṭabarī and Ibn al-ʿAthīr. This could be seen as a clear sign of man driven by an uncontrolled blind passion with little or no reflection on the disastrous consequences of such an act, the behavior of a leader who is more a *jāhil* rather than *ḥalīm*. It is therefore not surprising when seeing Ibn al-ʿAthīr's narration of Zīyād torturing Ṣayf b. Faṣil for his refusal to take part in the cursing of ʿAlī. The despotic tendency of the leader was reflected by his governors.[2]

Al-Balādhurī continues to narrate that there were still good people who were willing to change their minds once they were informed of the sincerity of Ḥujr's cause. Amongst these was Ibn Khuraym al-Murrī and ʿAbd al-Raḥmān b. al-Aswad b. ʿAbd Yaghūth al-Zuhrī who both rejected the responsibility of executing Ḥujr once they knew of his true beliefs.[3]

Ibn ʿAsākir's narration concerning Ḥujr's death clearly displays that there was a lack of *ḥilm* in Muʿāwiya's decision. Muʿāwiya asks for advice concerning the killing of Ḥujr. The advice however is taken from men whose very attitude to the incident is wreckless and bloodthirsty, with little concern for the consequences and more concern for their position before the caliph. A man of *ḥilm* would be seen as a man who would smother his feelings and be steady in his judgement. However, Muʿāwiya does not fit either description. While Ibn ʿAsākīr narrates that ʿAmr b. al-Aswad al-ʿAnsī left the decision in Muʿāwiya's hands by telling him that he knew the people of Iraq better than anybody else,[4] Muʿāwiya listens to two personalities. One is clearly more rash in his conclusion and gives a speech

1. Al-Balādhurī, *Ansāb*, vol. 4, 243; al-Yaʿqūbī, *Tārīkh*, vol. 4, 218; al-Ṭabarī, vol. 5, 253-4; Ibn al-ʿAthīr, *al-Kāmil*, vol. 3, 69-70.

2. Ibn al-ʿAthīr, *al-Kāmil,* vol. 3, 73.

3. Al-Balādhurī, *Ansāb*, vol. 4, 259-260.

4. Ibn ʿAsākīr, *Tārīkh Medinat Dimashq*, vol. 12, 223-224.

based on flattery than sincere advise. The second displays a hint of *ḥilm*. He is seeking to offer an avenue of support for Ḥujr where he seeks to make the caliph consider forgiveness as an option. The first is Abū Muslim al-Khawlānī, also known as ʿAbdullāh b. Thuwāb, who states:

> We have never hated you since we loved you, never disobeyed you since we obeyed you, never left you since we joined you, and never violated our oath of allegiance to you since we gave it. Our swords are on our shoulders; if you order us we will obey and if you call us we will heed.[1]

1. Ibn ʿAsākīr, *Tārīkh*, vol. 12, 224.

Bibliography

Primary Sources

Ibn ʿAbd al-Barr, Yūsuf b. ʿAbdullāh, *al-Istīʿāb fī maʿrifat al-aṣḥāb*, ed. A. al-Bajjāwī, 4 vols. (Cairo, n.d.).

Ibn ʿAbd al-Ḥakam, ʿAbd al-Raḥmān b. ʿAbd Allāh, *Futuḥ Miṣr wa-Akhbāruha* (Baghdad, 1967).

————————, *Futūḥ Miṣr* (al-Qāhirah: Maktabat al-Thaqāfah al-Dīnīyah, 1995).

Ibn Abī al-Ḥadīd, ʿIzz al-Dīn Abū Ḥamīd, *Sharḥ Nahjul Balāgha* (Cairo: Dār al-kutub al-ʿArabīyyah, 1944).

Ibn ʿAbd Rabbihī, Aḥmad b. Muḥammad, *al-ʿIqd al-farīd*, ed. Aḥmad Amīn, Aḥmad al-Zayn and Ibrāhīm al-Ibyārī (Cairo: Lajnat al-Ta'lif wa al-Tarjama wa al-Nashr, 1948).

ʿAlam al-Hudā, al-Sharīf Abū l-Qāsim ʿAlī b. al-Husain al-Murtaḍā aka Dhūl-Majdain, "*Majmu'a fi funūn min ʿilm al-kalām*" in *Nafā'is al-*

makhṭūṭāt, ed. Muḥammad Ḥasan Āl-Yāsīn, 1st edition (Baghdād: al-Ma'arif, 1955).

________, "*al-Uṣūl al-itiqaḍīyya*" in *Nafā'is al-makhṭūṭāt*, ed. Muḥammad Ḥasan Āl-Yāsīn, 1st edition (Baghdād: al-Ma'ārif, 1955).

________, *al-Shāfī fil Imāma* (Tehran, 1301/1884).

al-Amīnī, 'Abd al-Ḥusayn, *al-Ghadeer* (Beirut: Dār al Kitāb al-'Arabī, 1970).

________, *al-Ghadīr fil Kitāb wal Sunnah wal Adab* (Qum: Furū al-Dīn Publishers, 1995).

Asadābādī, 'Abd al-Jabbār b. Aḥmad, *Fīraq wa-ṭabaqāt al-mu'tazilah* (Cairo: Dār al-Ṭibā'ah al-Jāmi'īyah, 1972).

________, *al-Mughnī* (Cairo: al-Mu'assasa al-Miṣrīyya al-'āmma lil-ta'līf wal-anbā' wal-nashr, 1961-5).

Ibn 'Asākir, 'Alī b. al-Ḥasan, *Ta'rīkh Madīnat Dimashq*, ed. Muḥibb al-Dīn Abī Sa'īd 'Umar b. Gharāma al-'Amrawī (Beirut: Dār al-Fikr, 1995-1998).

al-Ash'ārī, Abū al-Ḥasan 'Alī b. Ismā'īl, *Kitāb al-Ibānah 'an uṣūl al-diyānah* (Hyderabad: 1321/1903); tr. by W.C. Klein as *The Elucidation of Islam's Foundation* (New Haven: 1940).

________, Abū al-Ḥasan Alī b. Ismā'īl, *Kitāb al-Luma'*, text and translation in R. J. McCarthy, *The Theology of al-Ash'arī* (Beirut: 1953).

________, *Maqālāt al-Islāmiyyīn*, ed. Hellmut Ritter (Istanbul, 1928).

al-ʿAsqalānī, Aḥmad b. ʿAlī Ibn Ḥajar, *al-Iṣābah fī tamyīz al-ṣaḥābah* (Cairo: Būlāq, 1328/1910).

__________, *Lisān al-mīzān* (Beirut: Dār al-Fikr, 1987-1988).

__________, *Tahdhīb al-Tahdhīb fī rijāl al-ḥadīth* (Beirut, 1968).

Ibn Aʿtham, *Kitāb al-Fūtūḥ*, 8 vols. (Ḥaydarabād: Dā'irat al-Maʿārif al-ʿUthmānīyyah, 1968-75).

__________, Muḥammad b. ʿAlī, *Kitāb al-Futūḥ*, Istanbul Manuscript, Library of Ahmet III.

Ibn al-ʿAthīr, Izz al-Dīn, *al-Bāhir fī Tārīkh ad-Dawllah al-Tatabanya,* ed. A. Tulaymat (Cairo: 1962).

__________, *al-Kāmil fi al-ta'rīkh*, ed. C.J. Tornberg (Leiden: Brill, 1868-70).

__________, *al-Kāmil fī al-Tārīkh* (Beirut, 1965).

al-Baghdādī, Abū Manṣūr ʿAbd al-Qāhir Tāhir, *Uṣūl al-dīn* (Istānbūl: Madrasat al-Ilāhīyāt bi-Dār al-Funūn al-Tūrkīyah, 1928), simplified translation in H.A.R. Gibb, "Constitutional Organisation" in *Law in the Middle East*, ed. Majid Khadduri and Herbert J. Liebesny (Washington D.C., 1955).

al-Balādhurī, *Ansāb al-Ashrāf* (published for the first time by the School of Oriental Studies, Hebrew University, Jerusalem, SDF Goitein Univ Press, 1936).

__________, *Ansāb al-Ashrāf*, ed. Muḥammad Bāqir al-Maḥmūdī (Beirut, 1974).

———, Aḥmed b. Yaḥyā, *Ansāb al-Ashrāf*, ed. Iḥsān ʿAbbās (Wiesbaden: Franz Steiner, 1979).

———, *Ansāb al-Ashrāf* (Beirut: Dār al-Fikr, 1996).

———, *Futūḥ al-Buldān*, ed. M. de Goeje (Leiden: Brill, 1865).

Al-Bāqillānī, Abū Bakr Muḥammad b. al-Ṭayyib, *Manāqib al-aʿimmah al-arbaʿah,* ed. Samīra Farhat (Beirut: Dār al-Muntakhab al-ʿArabī, 2002).

———, *al-Tamhīd fi al-Radd ʿalā al-mulḥidah al-muʿaṭṭalah wa al-rāfiḍah wa-l-Khawārij wa-l-Muʿtazilah* (al-Qāhirah: Dār al-Fikr al-Islāmī, 1947).

al-Dīnawarī, Ābu Ḥanīfah Āḥmad b. Dawūd, *al-Akhbār al-ṭiwāl* (Leiden: 1888).

al-Farazdaq, Hammām b. Ghālib Abū Firās, *Dīwān*, ed. M.I.A. al-Ṣāwī (Cairo, 1936 and Beirut, 1960).

Hajjī Khalīf, Muṣṭafā b. ʿAbdullāh, *Kashf al-ẓunūn ʿan asāmī al-kutub wa-al-funūn,* ed. Gustav Flugel, 7 vols. (Leipzig and London: 1835-58).

al-Ḥamawī, Yāqūt b. ʻAbdallāh, *Irshād al-arīb ilā ma'rifat al-adīb: al-Muʿjam al-ʿUdaba* (Dictionary of Learned Men), ed. D.S. Margoliouth, 7 vols., 2nd edition (London: 1923-31).

Ibn Ḥanbal, ʿAbd Allāh b. Aḥmad, *Musnad* (Cairo: Maymanya Publishers, 1313 AH).

Ibn Hishām, Muḥammad b. Aḥmad, *Ṣīrāt Sayyidna Muḥammad Rasūl Allāh*, ed. Ferdinand Wüstenfeld, 2 vols. (Göttingen, 1858-60; reprint, Frankfurt am Main, 1961).

al-Jāḥiẓ, Abū ʿUthmān ʿAmr b. Baḥr, *al-Bayān wa'l-tabyīn*, ed. A.S.M. Harun (Cairo, 1948-50).

________, *Kitab al-hayawān*, ed, A.S.M. Harun, 2nd edition (Cairo: Muṣṭafā al-Bābī al-Ḥalabī, 1965-1969).

________, *Rasā'il al-Jāḥiẓ*, ed. H. al-Sandubi (Cairo: Yuṭlab min al-Maktabah al-Tijārīyah al-Kubrā, 1933).

________, *Rasa'il al-Jāḥiẓ*, ed. A.S.M. Harun (Cairo, 1965).

________, *Risālat al-ʿUthmānīyya*, ed. A.S.M. Harun (Cairo: Dār al-Kitāb al-ʿArabī, 1955).

al-Jumaḥī, Muḥammad b. Sallām, *Ṭabaqāt fuḥūl al-shuʿarā'*, ed. A. M. Shakir (Cairo, 1952).

al-Juwaynī, ʿAbd al-Malik b. ʿAbd Allāh b. Yūsuf, *Ghiyāth al-Umām fi al-Tiyāth al-Ẓulam*, ed. A. Dīb (Qatar, 1400/1979).

Ibn Kathīr, Ismāʿīl b. ʿUmar, *al-Bidāyah wa al-Nihāyah* (Beirut: Maktabah al-Maʿārif, 1966).

________, *al-Bidāya wa-l-nihāya*, ed. ʿAlī ʿAbd al-Ṣāṭir (Beirut: Dār al-Kutub al-ʿIlmiyyah, 1985).

Ibn Khaldūn, *Muqaddimah* (Cairo, 1321), quoted by L. Gardet and M.M. Anawati in *Introduction à La Théologie Musulmane* (Paris: Librairie Philosophique J. Vrin, 1948).

Ibn Khallikān, Shams al-Dīn Abū al-ʿAbbās Aḥmad b. Muḥammad, *Wafayāt al-A'yān*, (Cairo, 1948).

al-Khaṭafā, Jarīr b. ʿAṭīyya b., *Diwān*, ed. M.I.A. al-Ṣāwī (Cairo 1353) and ed. N.M.A. Ṭāhā (Cairo 1969-70).

Ibn al-Khayyāṭ, ʿAbd al-Raḥīm b. Muḥammad, *Kitāb al-Intiṣar wa-al-radd ʿala Ibn al-Rawandī al-mulḥid*, ed. and tr. Albert Nader (Beirut: al-Matbaʿah al-Kathulikiyah, 1957).

__________, *al-Ṭabaqāt: riwāyat Abī ʿImrān Mūsā al-Tustarī*, ed. Akram Ḍiyāʾ al-ʿUmarī (Baghdad: Maṭbaʿat al-ʿĀnī, 1967).

__________, *Tārīkh Khalīfah b. Khayyaṭ* (Beirut: Dār al-Kutub al-ʿIlmīyyah, 1995).

al-Kindī, Abū ʿUmar Muḥammad b. Yūsuf, *Kitāb al-Wulāt wa Kitāb al-Quḍāt*, ed. R. Guest (Leiden, 1912).

al-Isfahānī, Abū al-Faraj ʿAlī b. al-Ḥusayn, *Kitāb al-Aghānī* (Cairo, 1285).

__________, *Kitāb al-Aghānī*, ed. Naṣr al-Hurinī, 20 vols. (Bulāq, 1868).

__________, *Kitāb al-Aghānī* (Leiden, 1905).

__________, *Kitāb al-Aghānī* (Cairo, 1927-74).

__________, *Maqātil al-Ṭālibīyīn*, ed. Aḥmed Saqr (Cairo, 1949; 2nd edtn, Tehran, 1970).

———, *Maqatil al-Ṭālibiyyīn* (Najaf: al-Maktabah al-Ḥaydarīyah, 1965).

al-Isfahāni, Ḥasan Muḥammad al-Raghib, *Kitāb al-mufradāt fī gharīb al-Qurʾān* (Beirut: Dār al-maʿrifah, n.d.).

al-Jaṣṣāṣ, Aḥmad b. ʿAlī al-Rāzī, *Uṣūl al-fiqh al-musammā bi al-Fuṣūl fī al-uṣūl,* 4 vols., ed. U.J. Nashmī (Kuwait: Wizārat al-Awqāf, 1994).

Mālik b. Anas, *Muwaṭṭa' al-Imām Mālik b. Anas* (Jeddah: Dār al-Shurūq, 1985).

Ibn Manẓūr, Muḥammad b. Mukarram, *Lisān al-ʿArab*, 20 vols. (Cairo: Būlaq, 1300-108 AH).

al-Maqrīzī, Ahmad b. ʿAlī, *al-Khiṭaṭ*, ed. G. Wiet (Cairo, 1911-2).

al-Maṣrī, Imām Jamāl al-Dīn b. Manẓūr, *Lisān al-ʿArab* (Beirut: Dār Ṣādir, 1955-56).

al-Masʿ ūdī, ʿAlī b. al-Ḥusayn, *Murūj al-Dhahāb wa Maʿādin al-Jawhar*, ed. C. Pellat (Beirut: Université Libanaise, 1966-79).

———, *Les Prairies d'or,* ed and trans. Barbier de Maynard and Pavet de Courteille, 9 vols. (Paris, 1861-77).

———, ʿAlī b. al-Ḥusayn, *al-Tanbīḥ wa-l-ishrāf* (Leiden, 1894, rpt., Beirut: Maktabat al-Khayyāṭ, 1965).

al-Marzubānī, Abī ʿUbayd Allāh Muḥammad b. ʿImrān b. Mūsā, *al-Muwashshah* (Cairo, 1924).

al-Māwardī, Abū al-Ḥasan ʿAlī b. Muḥammad b. Ḥabīb, *al-Aḥkām al-Sulṭānīyyah* (Egypt, 1966).

al-Minqārī, Naṣr b. Muzaḥim, *Waq'at Ṣiffīn,* ed. A.S.M. Harūn (Cairo, 1365 AH).

———, *Waq'at Ṣiffīn*, ed. A.S.M. Harun (Cairo, 1382 AH).

al-Mufaḍḍal b. Salamah, *Fākhīr*, ed. C.A. Storey (Leyden: Brill, 1915).

al-Mufīd, Abū Abdullāh Muḥammad b. Muḥammad, *Awā'il al-maqālāt fi'l-madhāhib al-mukhtārāt*, ed. 'Abbāsqūlī S. Wajdī, with notes and introduction by Fazl Allāh Zanjānī, 2nd edition (Tabriz: Charandabi, 1371).

———, *al-Fuṣūl al-mukhtārah min al-'uyūn wa-al-maḥāsin* (Tehran: Intishārāt-i Navīd, 1983).

———, *al-Ifṣāh fi Imāmat Amīr al-Mu'minīn 'Alī b. Abī Ṭalib*, 2nd edition (Najaf: al-Haidariyya, 1950).

———, *Kitāb al-Irshād*, tr. I.K.A. Howard (London: The Muḥammadi Trust, 1981).

———, *Sharḥ 'aqā'id al-Ṣadūq* (Beirut: Dār al-Kitāb al-Islāmī, 1983).

———, *Taṣḥīh al-i'tiqād* (Qum, 1951).

Ibn al-Murtaḍā, Aḥmad b. Yaḥyā, *Ṭabaqāt al-Mu'tazila/Die Klassen der Mu'taziliten von Ibn al-Murtaḍā*, ed. Sussana Diwald-Wilzer (Beirut: Imrimerie Catholique, 1961), as cited in L. Clarke, *Shī'ite Heritage*.

al-Najāshī, Abī al-'Abbās Aḥmad b. 'Alī, *Rijāl al-Najāshī* (Beirut: Dār al-Adwā', 1988).

al-Nīsābūrī, Muḥammad b. ʿAbd Allāh al-Ḥakīm, *al-Mustadrak ala l-Ṣaḥīḥayn* (India: Dā'irat al-Maʿārif al-Nād'imiyet al-Qā'ima fī l-Hind, 1913).

al-Nūmairī, Abū Zaid ʿUmar Ibn Shabba b. ʿAbida Zaid, *Tārīkh al-Madīna al-Munawarrah*, ed. Fahīm Muḥammad Shaltūt (Iran, 1989).

Nuwayrī, Aḥmad b. ʿAbd al-Wahhāb, *Nihāyat al-ʿArab fī funūn al-Adāb* (Cairo, 1342-48).

Al-Qāḍī al-Nuʿmān, Abū Ḥanīfa al-Nuʿmān b. Abī ʿAbdillah Muḥammad b. Manṣūr al-Tamīmī, *Daʿaʿim al-Islam*, ed. A.A. Fyzee, 2 vols. (Cairo, 1951-60).

Qāsim b. Sallām, Abū ʿUbayd, *Kitāb al-amwāl* (al-Qāhirah: Dār al-Fikr, 1975).

al-Qurashī, Yaḥyā b. Adam, *Kitāb al-Kharāj*, ed. Th. W. Juynboll (Leiden: E.J. Brill, 1896).

Ibn Qutayba, ʿAbdullāh b. Muslim, *al-Imāmāh wa'l-siyāsah* (Cairo, 1909).

__________, *Kitāb al-maʿarif*, ed. Tharwat ʿUkāshah (Cairo: Maṭbaʿat Dār al-Kutub, 1960).

Ibn Sa'd, Muḥammad, *al-Ṭabaqāt al-kubrā* (Beirut, 1947-60).

al-Ṣafadī, Khalīl b. Aybak, *al-Wāfī bi-al-wafayāt* (Beirut: Dār Iḥyā' al-Turāth al-ʿArabī, 2000).

al-Sanʿānī, ʿAbd al-Razzāq b. Ḥammām, *Muṣannaf*, ed. Ḥabīb al-Raḥmān al-Aʿẓamī, 11 vols. (Simlak, Dahbel/Beirut, 1391/1972).

Ibn Shahrāshūb, Rashīd al-Dīn Abī Ja'far Muḥammad b. 'Alī, *Kitāb Ma'ālim al-'ulamā'* (Ṭehrān: Maṭba'at Fardīn, 1934).

al-Shammākhī, Abū al-'Abās Aḥmad b. Sa'īd, *Kitāb al-Siyār* (Cairo, 1301).

al-Shīrāzī, Abū Isḥāq, *al-Ishārah ilā madhhab Ahl al-ḥaqq* (al-Qāhirah: Markaz al-Sīrah wa al-Sunnah, 1999).

al-Sijistānī, Abū Ya'qūb Isḥāq b. Aḥmad, *Kitāb al-Iftikhār,* ed. with notes and comments by Ismail K. Poonawala (Beirut: Dār al-Gharb al-Islāmī, 2000).

al-Ṭabarī, Abū Ja'far Muḥammad b. Jarīr b.Yazīd, *Ta'rīkh al-Rusul wal-mulūk,* ed. M.J. de Goeje, et al. (Leiden: Brill, 1881).

———, *Tārīkh al-Rusūl wal-Mulūk* (Cairo: al-Istiqāma Publishers, 1939).

———, *Tārīkh al-rusul wa-al-mulūk,* ed. Muḥammad Abū al-Faḍl Ibrāhīm, 11 vols. (Cairo: Dār al-Ma'ārif, 1960-1970).

———, *Tārīkh al-Rusul wal-Mulūk,* 13 vols. (Beirut: Dār al-Fikr, 1998).

al-Tabrīzī, Yaḥyā b. 'Alī Khaṭīb, *Sharḥ al-Ḥamāsah* (Cairo, 1916), vol. 1, 3.

al-Tamīmī, Sayf b. 'Umar al-Asadī, *Kitāb al-Ridda wa'l-futūh and Kitāb al-jamal wa-masīr 'Ā'isha wa-'Alī: A Facsimile Edition of the Fragments Preserved in the University Library of Imām Muḥammad Ibn Sa'ud Islamic University in Riyadh* (Leiden: Smitskamp Oriental Antiquarium, 1995).

al-Tawḥīdī, Abū Ḥayyān ʿAlī b. Muḥammad, *al-Baṣā'ir wa-al-dhakhā'ir*, ed. Wadād al-Qāḍī (Beirut, 1988).

__________, *Kitāb al-imtāʿ wa-al-mu'ānasah*, ed. Aḥmed Amīn and Aḥmed al-Zayn (Cairo, 1953).

__________, *Risālat al-Saqīfah*, published in I. al-Kīlānī, ed., *Thalāth rasā'il lī-Abī Ḥayyān al-Tawḥīdī* (Damascus, 1951).

Ibn al-Ṭiqṭaqā, *al-Fakhrī fī al-adab al-sulṭānīyah wal duwal al-islāmīyya* (Cairo: al-Maktaba al-tijariya al-kubrā, 1927).

Ibn Ṭūlūn, Muḥammad b. ʻAlī, *Quḍāt Dimashq: al-thaghr al-bassām fī dhikr man wuliyya qaḍā' al-Shām*, ed. S. Munajjid (Damascus, 1956).

al-Ṭusī, *al-Fihrist*, ed. A. Sprenger/new ed. Maḥmud Ramyar (Mashhad, 1351).

Yaʿqūb, Abū Yūsuf, *Kitāb al-Kharāj* (1886).

al-Yaʿqūbī, Aḥmad b. Abī Yaʿqūb, *Kitāb al-Tārīkh* (Leiden: Brill, 1883).

__________, "Kitab al-Buldan" in Ibn Rustah's *A'lāq al-nafīsah*, ed. M.J. de Goeje (Leiden: Brill, 1892).

al-Zubayrī, Abī ʿAbd Allāh al-Muṣʿab b. ʿAbd Allāh b. al-Muṣʿab, *Nasab Quraysh* (Cairo: Dār al-Maʿārif lil-Ṭibāʿah wa-al-Nashr, 1953).

Secondary Sources

Abbott, N., *Studies in Arabic Literary Papyri* (Chicago: University of Chicago Press, 1957).

al-ʿAdawī, Ibrāhīm Aḥmad, *al-Dawla al-Umawīyah* (Cairo: Maktabat al-Shabāb, 1987-88).

Afsaruddin, Asma, *Excellence and Precedence: Medieval Discourse on Legitimate Leadership* (Leiden: Brill, 2002).

__________, *The First Muslims: History and Memory* (Oxford: Oneworld Publications, 2008).

__________, "In Praise of the Caliphs: Recreating History from the *Manāqib* Literature", *IJMES*, 31 (1999).

Ahlwardt, W., *The Divans of the Six Ancient Arabic Poets*, 25, no. 23:11 (London, 1870).

ʿAlī, Jawād, "Mawarid *Tārīkh* al-Ṭabarī", *Majallat al-Majmaʿ al-ʿIlmī al-Iraqī*, 1 (1950).

al-ʿAlī, Ṣalih, "Muslim Estates in Ḥijāz in the First Century", *JESHO*, vol. 2 (1959).

ʿAlī, ʿAbdullāh Yūsuf, tr. *The Qur'ān* (New York: Tahrike Tarsile Qur'an, Inc., 2007).

Allard, M., *Le Probleme des attributs divins dans la doctrine d'al-Ashari et de ses premiers grands disciples* (Beirut, 1965).

Aqīl, Nabil, *Dirasat fi al-ʿaṣr al-umawī,* 4th edition (Damascus: University of Damascus Press, 1991-92).

ʿArafāt, W., "The Historical Background to the Elegies on ʿUthmān b. ʿAffān Attributed to Ḥassan b. Thabit", *BSOAS,* 33 (1970).

Arberry, A. J., *Arabic Poetry: A Primer for Students* (Cambridge, Cambridge University Press, 1965).

Arnold, T. W., *The Caliphate* (New York : Barnes and Noble, 1966 [1924]).

al-ʿAskarī, S. M. *The Role of ʿĀʾisha in the History of Islam: ʿĀʾisha in the Time of Muʿāwiya b. Abī Sufyān,* tr. Dr. ʿAlāʾ al-Dīn Pārzārgādī (Iran: Naba Organization, 2000).

Ashtiany, J. and J.D. Latham,ʿ*Abbāsid Belles-Lettres* (Cambridge: Cambridge University Press, 1990).

ʿAṭwān, Ḥusayn, *Niẓām wilayāt al-ʿahd wa wirathāt al-khilāfah fī al-ʿasr al-Umawī* (Beirut: Dār al-Jīl, 1991).

ʿAẓamī, M. M., *On Schacht's Origins of Muḥammadan Jurisprudence* (Oxford: Oxford Centre for Islamic Studies; 1996).

________, *Studies in Early Ḥadith Literature* (Indianapolis: American Trust Publications, 1992).

al-Azmeh, A., *Muslim Kingship* (New York: I.B. Tauris Publishers, 1997).

Bahar, Muḥammad Taqī, ed., *Tārīkh-i Sīstān* (Tehran, 1314).

Bakhit, M. Adnan, and Robert Schick, eds., *The History of the Bilād al-Shām During the Umayyad Period: Fourth International Conference of the History of Bilād al-Shām* (Amman: University of Jordan and Yarmouk University, 1989).

Bakhtin, M. M., *The Dialogic Imagination*, ed. Michael Holquist (Austin: Univeristy of Texas Press, 1981).

Barthes, Roland, *The Pleasure of the Text* New York: Hill and Wang, 1975).

Bashear, Suliman, "The Title Fārūq and its Association with ʿUmar I", *Studia Islamica*, 72 (1990).

Bates, Michael, "The ʿArab-Byzantine Bronze Coinage of Syria: An Innovation by ʿAbd al-Mālik", *A Colloquium in Memory of George Carpenter Miles* (New York: American Numismatic Society, 1976).

Bayhom-Daou, T., "The Imām's Knowledge and the Qurʾān According to al-Faḍl b. Shādhān al-Nīsābūrī (d. 260 A.H./874 A.D.)", *BSOAS*, 64, 2 (2001).

______, *Shaykh Mufīd: Makers of the Muslim World* (Oxford: Oneworld, 2005).

Berg, H., *The Development of Exegesis in Early Islam* (Richmond: Curzon Press, 2000).

Birkeland, H., *Old Muslim Opposition Against Interpretation of the Qurʾān* (Oslo: Jacob Dybwad, 1955).

Brock, Sebastian P., "Syriac Sources for Seventh Century History", *BMGS*, 2 (1976).

________, "Syriac Views of Emergent Islam' in G.H.A. Juynboll (ed.), *Studies in the First Century of Islamic Society* (Carbondale and Edwardsville, 1982).

Brockelmann, C., "al-Ya'kubī", *Encyclopaedia of Islam*, 2nd edition (Leiden: Brill, 1954-66).

Brown, J., *Ḥādīth: Muḥammad's Legacy in the Medieval and Modern World* (Oxford: Oneworld Publications, 2009).

Burton, J., *An Introduction to the Ḥadīth* (Edinburgh: Edinburgh University Press, 1994).

Busse, H., "Monotheismus und Islamische Christologie in der Bauinschrift des Felsendoms in Jerusalem", *Theologische Quartalschrift*, 161 (1981) as cited by Donner in *Narratives of Islamic Origins.*

Cahen, C., "History and Historians: From the Beginnings to the Time of al-Ṭabarī", *Religion, Learning and Science in the 'Abbāsid Period: The Cambridge History of Arabic Literature* (Cambridge: Cambridge University Press, 1990).

Calder, Norman, "The Qurrā and the Arab Lexicographical Tradition", *JSS*, 36, 2 (1991).

Cameron, A. J., *Abū Dharr al-Ghifārī: An Examination of His Image in the Hagiography of Islam*, Oriental Translation Fund, New Series, vol. 63 (London: Luzac and Co. Ltd. for the Royal Asiatic Society, 1973).

Cameron, Averil, "Images of Authority: Elites and Icons in Late Sixth-Century Byzantium", in M. Mullet and R. Scott (eds.), *Byzantium and the Classical Tradition* (Birmingham: University of Birmingham Press, 1981).

el-Cheikh, N., *Byzantium Viewed by the Arabs* (Cambridge, MA: Harvard Centre for Middle-Eastern Studies, 2004).

Cooperson, M., *Classical Arabic Biography* (Cambridge: Cambridge University Press, 2000).

Crone, Patricia, *God's Rule: Government in Islam* (New York: Columbia University Press, 2004).

__________, *Meccan Trade and the Rise of Islam* (Piscataway, NJ: Gorgias Press, 2004).

__________, *Slaves on Horses: The Evolution of the Islamic Polity* (Cambridge: Cambridge University Press, 1980).

__________, "Were the Qays and Yemen of the Umayyad Period Political Parties?" *DI*, 71 (1994).

Crone, Patricia, and M. Cook, *Hagarism: The Making Of The Islamic World* (Cambridge: Cambridge University Press, 1977).

Crone, Patricia, and F.W. Zimmerman, *The Epistle of Sālim b. Dhakwān* (New York: Oxford University Press, 2001).

Coulson, N.J., *A History of Islamic Law, Islamic Surveys,* vol. 2 (Edinburgh: Edinburgh University Press, 1964; reprint, 1991).

Culler, Jonathan, *The Pursuit of Signs: Semiotics, Literature, Deconstruction* (London: Routledge & Kegan Paul, 1981).

Dabashi, Hamid, *Authority in Islam: From the Rise of Muḥammad to the Establishment of the Umayyads,* 2nd edition (New Brunswick, NJ: Transaction Books, 1992).

Dakake, Maria, *The Charismatic Community: Shīʿite Identity in Early Islam* (Albany: SUNY Press, 2007).

al-Dīb, ʿAbd al-ʿAẓīm, *Imām al-Ḥāramayn* (Kuwait: Dār al-Qalam, 1981).

Dixon, A. A., *The Umayyad Caliphate 65-86/684-705: A Political Study* (London: Luzac, 1971).

Donner, Fred, *The Early Islamic Conquests* (Princeton: Princeton University Press, 1981).

__________, "From Believers to Muslims: Confessional Self-Identity in the Early Islamic Community" in *The Byzantine and Early Islamic Near East, IV: Patterns of Communal Identity,* ed. Lawrence I. Conrad (Princeton: Darwin Press, 2003).

__________, *Narratives of Islamic Origins: The Beginning of Islamic Historical Writing* (Princeton: The Darwin Press, Inc: 1998).

Dūrī, A. A., *The Rise of History Among the Arabs* (Princeton: Princeton University Press, 1983).

Elad, A., "The Beginnings of Historical Writing by the Arabs: The Earliest Syrian Writers on the Arab Conquests", *JSAI*, 28 (2003).

Ennami, A. K., "A Description of New ʿIbādī Manuscripts from North Africa", *Journal of Semitic Studies*, 15 (1970).

Farouq, Umar, *Khalīfah b. Khayyaṭ Muʿarrikhān* (Baghdād: 1967).

Faris, N. A., "Development in Arab Historiography as Reflected in the Struggle Between ʿAlī and Muʿāwiyah" in *Historians of the Middle*

East, ed. P. M. Holt and B. Lewis (Oxford: Oxford University Press, 1962).

Flood, Gavin, *Beyond Phenomenology: Rethinking the Study of Religion* (London: Cassell, 1999).

Fowden, G., *Quṣayr ʿAmra: Art and the Umayyad Elite in Late Antique Syria* (Berkeley: University of California Press, 1st Edition, 2004).

Fück, Johann, "Die Rolle des Traditionalismus im Islam", *Zeitschrift der Deutschen Morgenlandischen Gesellschaft*, 93 (1939) in Berg, H., *The Development of Exegesis in Early Islam*, (Richmond: Curzon Press, 2000).

Fyzee, A. A., "Qāḍī an-Nuʿmān: The Fāṭimid Jurist and Author", *JRAS* (1934).

Geyer, R., *The Divan of al-ʿĀʾisha* (London, E.J.W. Gibb Memorial series, N.S.6, 1928).

Gleave, R. "Between Ḥadīth and Fiqh: Early Imāmī Collections of Akhbār", *ILS*, 8, 3 (2001).

Goldziher, I., *Mohamedanische Studien* (first published 1890), vol. 2, tr. into English by C.R. Barber and S.M. Stern under the title *Muslim Studies*, vol. 2 (London: George Allen & Unwin, 1967-71).

———, *The Principles of Law in Islam*, vol. 8, 301, in *The Historian's History of the World*, ed. H.S. Williams (London, 1907).

Goriawala, M., *A Descriptive Catalogue of the Fyzee collection of Ismaili Manuscripts*, no. 24 and no. 49 entitled *Ithbāt al-Imāmah* (Bombay: University of Bombay, 1965).

Gorke, A., "The Historical Tradition about al-Hudaybīyya", in *The Biography of Muḥammad: The Issue of the Sources*, ed. Harald Motzki (Leiden: Brill, 2000).

Gruendler, B., "Verse and Taxes: The Function of Poetry in Selected Literary *Akhbār* of the Third/Ninth Century" in *On Fiction and Adab in Medieval Arabic Literature*, ed. Ph. F. Kennedy (Wiesbaden: Harrassowitz, 2005).

Gunther, S., "Assessing the Sources of Classical Arabic Compilations: The Issue of Categories and Methodologies", *BJMES*, 32, 1 (2005).

Halm, Heinz, *Shīʿism* (Edinburgh, 1992).

Hamda, Muḥammad Māhir, *Dirāsa wathā'iqīyya li-l-Tārīkh al-Islamī wa-maṣadirihī; min ʿahd banī umayyah ḥata al-fatḥ al-ʿUthmānī li-Sūriyah wa-Miṣr 40-922 AH /661-1516 CE* (Beirut: Mu'assassat al Risāla, 1988).

Hasson, Isaac, 'La conversion de Muʿāwiya b. Abī Sufyān', *JSAI*, 22 (1998).

Hawting, Gerald R., *The First Dynasty of Islam* (London: Routledge, 2000).

__________, "The Origins of the Muslim Sanctuary at Mecca", in G.H.A. Juynboll (ed.), *Studies on the First Century of Islamic Society* (Carbondale and Edwardsville, 1982).

________, "The Significance of the Slogan *La Ḥukma illa Lillah* and the References to the *Ḥudūd* in the Traditions about the *Fitna* and the Murder of ʿUthmān", *BSOAS*, 41 (1978).

el-Ḥibrī, T., *JSTOR*, vol. 118, n.1.

———, *Reinterpreting Islamic Historiography: Harūn al-Rashīd and the Narrative of the 'Abbāsid Caliphate* (Cambridge: Cambridge University Press, 1999).

Hinds, Martin, "The Banners and the Battle Cries of the Arabs at the Battle of Ṣiffīn (657 AD)", *al-Abḥāth*, 24 (1971).

———, "Mu'āwiya I", *The Encyclopaedia of Islam*, New Edition (Leiden: Brill, 1993).

———, "The Murder of the Caliph 'Uthmān", *IJMES*, 3 (1972).

———, "Sayf b. 'Umar's Sources on Arabia", *Studies in the History of Arabia*, 1: ii (1979).

———, "The Siffin Arbitration Agreement", *JSS*, 17 (1972).

Hitti, Philip K., *History of the Arabs* (Basingstoke: Palgrave Macmillan, 2002).

Hodgson, Marshall, "How Did the Early Shi'a become Sectarian", *JAOS*, 75 (1955).

Horst, Heribert, *Die Gewahrsmanner im korankommentar at-Ṭabarī: Ein Beitrag zur kenntnis der exegetischen Uberlieferung im Islam* (Rheinische Friedrich-Willhelms-Universitat zu Bonn, Ph.D dissertation, 1951) in Berg, H., *The Development of Exegesis in Early Islam* (Richmond: Curzon Press, 2000).

Hoyland, R., "Sebeos, the Jews and the Rise of Islam", *SMJR*, 2 (1996).

______, *Seeing Islam as Others Saw It* (Princeton: Darwin Press, 1997), quoting George of Resh'aina, "An Early Syriac Life of Maximus XXIII".

Humphreys, R. S., *Islamic History: A Framework for Inquiry* (Princeton: Princeton University Press, 1991).

______, *Muʿāwiya b. Abī Sufyān: From Arabia to Empire* (Oxford: Oneworld Publications, 2006).

Ibrāhīm, Maḥmood, *Merchant Capital and Islam* (Austin: The University of Texas Press, 1990).

______, *The Social and Economic Background of the Umayyad Caliphate* (University of California, Los Angeles, Ph.d. dissertation, 1981).

Ivanow, V., "Early Shī'ite Movements", *JBBRAS* (1941).

Izutsu, T., *Ethico-Religious Concepts in the Qurʾān* (Montreal: McGill University Press, 1966).

______, *God and Man in the Koran: Semantics of the Qurʾānic Weltanschauung* (Tokyo: The Keio Institute of Cultural and Linguistic Studies, 1964).

al-Jabburī, K. S., *Nuṣūs min Tārīkh Abī Mikhnaf Lūṭ b. Yaḥyā b. Sa'īd al-Jāmidī al-Azdī l-Kūfī l-Mutawaffa* [157 H] (Beirut: Dār al-Rasūl al-Akram, 1999).

Jones, J.M.B., "The Chronology of the *Maghāzī*: A Textual Survey", *BSOAS*, XIX (1957).

Juynboll, G.H.A., *Muslim Tradition: Studies in Chronology, Provenance and the Authorship of Early Ḥadīth* (Cambridge: Cambridge University Press, 1983).

______, *Studies on the First Century of Islamic Society* (Carbondale, IL: Southern Illinois University Press, 1982).

Kaegi, Walter, "Initial Byzantine Reactions to the Arab Conquests", *CH*, 38 (1969).

Kassis, H. E., *A Concordance of the Qurʾān* (Berkeley: The University of California Press, 1983).

Kennedy, Hugh, *The Prophet and the Age of the Caliphate: The Islamic Near East from the Sixth to the Eleventh Century* (London: Longman, 1986).

______, *Al-Ṭabarī: Studies in Late Antiquity and Early Islam* (London: Darwin Press, 2008).

Keshk, Khaled, *The Depiction of Muʿāwiya in the Early Islamic Sources* (Chicago: University of Chicago, 2002).

______, *The Historian's Muʿāwiyah: The Depiction of Muʿāwiyah in the Early Islamic Sources* (Saarbrucken: VDM Verlag Dr Muller, 2008).

______, "The Historiography of an Execution: The Killing of Ḥujr b. ʿAdī ", *Journal of Islamic Studies* 19, 1 (January 2008).

Khālidī, T., *Arab Historical Thought in the Classical Period* (New York: Cambridge University Press, 1994).

______, *Images of Muḥammad* (New York: Doubleday, 2009).

Kohlberg, Etan, "Evolution of the Shīʿa", *JQ*, 27 (1983).

______, "From Imāmīyya to Ithnā-Asharīyya", *BSOAS*, 39 (1976).

______, "Imām and Community in the Pre-Ghayba Period", in *Authority and Political Culture in Shī'ism*, ed. Sa'īd Amīr Arjomand (Albany: State University of New York Press, 1988).

______, "The Term *Muhaddath in Twelver* Shī'ism", *Studio Orientalia D.H. Baneth Dedicata* (Jerusalem: Magnes Press, 1979).

Kristeva, Julia, *Desire in Language: A Semiotic Approach to Literature and Art* (New York: Columbia University Press, 1980).

Lalani, Arzina, *Early Shīʿī Thought: The Teachings of Imām Muḥammad al-Bāqir* (London: I.B. Tauris and the Institute of ʿIsmāʿīlī Studies, 2004).

Lambton, A., *State and Government in Medieval Islam* (Oxford: Oxford University Press, 1981).

Lammens, Henri, *Etudies sur le regne du Calife Omiyade Mo'awiya I* (Leipzig, 1908).

______, "Mu'āwiya", *The Encyclopaedia of Islam,* 2nd edition (Leiden: Brill, 1954-66).

Lapidus, Ira M., *A History of Islamic Societies* (Cambridge: Cambridge University Press, 1988).

______, "Knowledge, Virtue, and Action: The Classical Muslim Conception of *Adab* and the Nature of Religious Fulfillment in Islam" in *Moral Conduct and Authority: The Place of Adab in South Asian Islam,* ed. Barbara D. Metcalf (Berkeley: University of California Press, 1984).

______, 'The Separation of State and Religion in the Development of Early Islamic Society", *IJMES* 6 (1975).

Lassner, J., *Islamic Revolution and Historical Memory* (New Haven: American Oriental Society, 1986).

Lecker, Michael, "The Estates of ʿAmr b. al-Āṣ in Palestine: Notes on a New Negev Arabic Inscription", *BSOAS*, 52 (1989).

Leder, Stefan, "The Literary Use of the *Khabar*: A Basic Form of Historical Writing" in *The Byzantine and Early Islamic Near East I: Problems in the Literary Source Material*, ed. Averil Cameron and Lawrence I. Conrad (Princeton: The Darwin Press, 1992).

Lewinstein, K., *Journal of the American Oriental Society*, 121, 2 (2001).

Lindsay, J., *Ibn Asākīr and Early Islamic History* (Princeton: Darwin Press, 2001).

Macdonald, D. B., *Development of Muslim Theology: Jurisprudence and Constitutional Theory* (New York: Charles Scrb.er's Sons, 1903).

MacIntyre, Alasdair, *A History of Ethics* (London: Routledge & Kegan Paul, 1967).

McCarthy, R. J., "Al-Bāqillānī", *Encyclopaedia of Islam*, 2nd edition (Leiden: Brill, 1954-66).

______, *The Theology of al-Ashʿārī* (Beirut: 1953).

McCutcheon, Russell T., "General Introduction" in *The Insider/Outsider Problem in the Study of Religion*, ed. Russell T. McCutcheon (London: Cassell, 1999).

McDermott, Martin J., *The Theology of Shaykh al-Mufīd* (Beirut, 1978).

Madelung, Wilferd, *The Succession to Muḥammad* (Cambridge: Cambridge University Press, 1996).

Madelung, Wilferd, "Early Sunnī Doctrine Concerning Faith as Reflected in the Kitāb al-Imān of Abū 'Ubayd al-Qāsim b. Sallām" (d. 224/839), *SI*, 32 (1970).

________________, "The Hāshimīyāt of al-Kumayt and Hāshimī Shīʿism", *SI*, 70 (1989).

Margoliouth, D. S., *Lectures on Arab Historians* (Calcutta: University of Calcutta, 1930).

Marsham, Andrew, *Rituals of Islamic Monarchy, Accession and Succession in the First Muslim Empire* (Edinburgh: Edinburgh University Press, 2009).

Martensson, U., "Discourse and Historical Analysis: The Case of al-Ṭabarī's History of the Messengers and the Kings", 16 (2005).

Mattson, I., *JR*, 78, 2 (1998).

Miles, G. C., 'Early Islamic Inscriptions Near Ṭā'if in the Ḥijāz', *JNES*, 7 (1948).

Millward, W. G., "Al-Yaʿqūbī's Sources and the Question of Shīʿī Partiality", *Abr Nahrain*, 12 (1971-1972).

Modarressi, Hossein, *Crisis and Consolidation in the Formative Period of Shīʿite Islam: Abū Jaʿfar b. Qiba al-Rāzī and His Contribution to Imāmite Shīʾite Thought* (Princeton: Darwin Press, 1993).

__________, *Tradition and Survival: A Bibliographical Survey of Early Shīʾite Literature* (Oxford: Oneworld Publications, 2003).

Montgomery, J., "al-Jāḥiẓ" in *Dictionary of Literary Biography*, vol. 311: *Arabic Literary Heritage 500-925, ed.* S.M. Toorawa and M. Cooperson (Detroit: Layman, Brucoli & Clark, 2005).

__________, "Jāḥiẓʿs *Kitāb al-Bayan wa-l-Tabayin*", in Julia Bray (ed.), *Writing and Representation: (London: Muslim Horizons,* 2006).

__________, "Of Models and Amanuenses: The Remarks on the Qaṣīda in Ibn Qutaybah's *Kitāb al-Shiʿr wa-l-Shuʿarā*", in R. Hoyland and P. Kennedy (ed.), *Islamic Reflections, Arabic Musings: Studies in Honour of Alan Jones (Oxford:* Gibb Memorial Trust, 2004).

Morony, M., trans., *History of Ṭabarī: Between Civil Wars: The Caliphate of Muʾāwiyah*, vol. 18 (Albany: State University of New York Press, 1987).

__________, *Iraq after the Muslim Conquest* (Princeton: N.J.; Princeton University Press, 1984).

__________, *NES*, 59, 2 (2000).

Motzki, H., *The Biography of Muḥammad: The Issue of the Sources* (Leiden: Brill, 2000).

______, *Ḥadīth: Origins and Development* (Aldershot: Ashgate, 2004).

______, 'The *Muṣannaf* of ʿAbd al-Razzāq b. Ḥammām al-Sanʿānī as a Source of Authentic *Aḥādīth* of the First Century AH', *JNES*, 50 (1991).

Mubarak, Z., *al-Nathr al-Fannī* (Cairo, 1934).

Muir, W. *The Caliphate: Its Rise, Decline and Fall* (London: Religious Tract Society, 1891).

al-Najjar, M., *al-Dawla al-Umawīyya fi al-sharq* (Cairo, 1962).

Nallino, C. A., "Appunti sulla natura del 'Califatto' in genere e sul presunto 'Califatto ottomano'", in *Raccolta di scritti editi e inediti* (Rome, 1941) as cited in Watt, W. Montgomery,"God's Caliph: Qur'ānic Interpretations and Umayyad Claims", *Iran and Islam*, ed. C. E. Bosworth (Edinburgh: Edinburgh University Press, 1971).

Noth, A., and L. Conrad, *The Early Arabic Historical Tradition: A Source-Critical Study* (Princeton: Darwin Press, 1994).

Ostrogorsky, George, *History of the Byzantine State* (Oxford: Blackwell, 1968).

Palmer, A., S. Brock, and R. Hoyland, *The Seventh Century in the West-Syrian Chronicles* (Liverpool: Liverpool University Press, 1993).

Pellat, C., *The Life and Works of Jāḥiẓ: Translation of Selected Texts* (Berkeley: University of California Press, 1969).

Petersen, E., "ʿAlī and Mu'āwiya: The Rise of the Ummayad Caliphate 656-661", *Acta Orientalia*, 23 (1955).

________, *ʿAlī and Muʿāwiya* (Copenhagen: Munksgaard, 1964).

Poonawala, Ismail K., *Al-Qaḍī al-Numān and his Urjuza on the Imāmate* (University of California, Los Angeles, Ph.d. dissertation, 1970).

al-Qāḍī, Wadād, *Bishr b. Kubar al-Balawī; Namūdhaj min al-nathr al-fannī al-mubakkir fī al-Yaman* (Beirut: Dār al-Gharb al-Islamī, 1985).

________, "al-Raka'iẓ al-fikrīyyah fī naẓrat Abū Ḥayyān al-Tawḥīdī ilā l-mujtama", *al-Abḥāth*, 23 (1970).

________, "The Religious Foundation of Late Umayyad Ideology and Practice", *Saber Religioso y Poder Politico en el Islam: Actas del Simposio Internacional*, Granada, 15-18 octubre 1991 (Madrid, 1994).

________, "The Term 'Khalīfa' in Early Exegetical Literature", *DWI*, 28 (1988).

Quṭb, Sayyid, *Social Justice in Islam*, tr. John Hardie (New York: Octagon Books, 1970).

Quṭbuddin, T., "*Khuṭba*: The Evolution of Early Arabic Oration", in *Classical Arabic Humanities in their Own Terms: Festschrift for Wolfhart Heinrichs on his 65th Birthday*, ed. Beatrice Gruendler (Leiden: Brill Academic Publishers, 2008).

Reinink, G.J., "The Beginnings of Syriac Apologetic Literature in Response to Islam", *Oriens Christianus*, 77 (1993).

Richards, D. S., "Ibn al-Athīr and the Later Parts of the *Kāmil*: A Study for Aims and Methods" in *Medieval Historical Writing in the Christian and Islamic Worlds*, ed. D.O. Morgan (London: SOAS,

University of London, 1982).

Rippin, A., "Literary Analysis of the Qur'ān, *Tafsīr* and *Sīrah*: The Methodologies of John Wansborough" in *Approaches to Islam in Religious Studies*, ed. Richard C. Martin (Tucson: University of Arizona Press, 1985).

Robinson, C., *ʿAbd al-Mālik: Makers of the Muslim World* (Oxford: Oneworld Publications, 2007).

_______, *Islamic Historiography* (Cambridge: Cambridge University Press, 2003).

Robson, J., "The *Isnād* in Muslim Tradition", *Transactions of the Glasgow University Oriental Society*, 15 (1953-4).

Rosenthal, F. A., *Knowledge Trimuphant : The Concept of Knowledge in Medieval Islam* (Leiden: Brill, 1970).

_______, *History of Muslim Historiography* (Leiden: Brill, 1968).

_______, *The History of Ṭabarī* (Albany: State University of New York Press, 1989).

Rubin, Uri, "The Eye of the Beholder: The Life of Muḥammad As Viewed By the Early Muslims, A Textual Analysis", *Studies in Late Antiquity and Early Islam*, 8 (Princeton: The Darwin Press, 1995).

al-Sāmarrā'ī, Ibrahīm, *Fī al-Muṣṭalaḥ al-Islāmī* (Beirut: Dār al-Hadāthah, 1990).

Schoeler, G., *The Oral and the Written in Early Islam*, tr. Uwe Vagelpohl (London: Routledge, 2006).

Serjeant, R. B., "The Caliph 'Umar's Letters to Abū Musā and Mu'āwiya", *SS*, 24 (1984).

Sezgīn, F., *Geschichte des Arabesque Schriftums, Band I: Qur'ān Wissenschaften, ḥadith, Geschichte, Fīqh, Dogmatik, Mystik bis ca. 430 H*, tr. H. Berg (Leiden: E.J. Brill, 1967).

Sezgin, U., *Abū Mikhnaf: Ein Beitrag zur Historiographie des umaiya-dischen Ziet* (Leiden: Brill, 1971) as cited in C. Robinson.

Shaban, M. A., *The Abbasid Revolution* (London: Cambridge University Press, 1970).

______, *Islamic History: A New Interpretation A.D. 600-750* (Cambridge: Cambridge University Press, 1971).

Shahid, Irfan, *Byzantium and the Arabs in the Fifth Century* (Washington D.C., Dumbarton Oaks Research Library Collection, 1989).

______, *Byzantium and the Arabs in the Sixth Century* (Washington D.C. Dumbarton Oaks Research Library Collection, 1995).

______, *Byzantium and the Arabs in Late Antiquity* (Bruxelles: Byzantion, 2005).

Sharon, Moshe, "Notes on the Question of Legitimacy of Government in Islam", *IAO*, 10 (1980).

______, "The Umayyads as Ahl al-Bayt", *JSAI*, 14 (1992).

Shepard, W., "The Development of the Thought of Sayyid Quṭb as Reflected in Earlier and Later Editions of 'Social Justice in Islam'", *DWI*, 32 (1992).

———, "Sayyed Quṭb's Doctrine of Jaḥilīyya", *IJMES*, 35 (2003).

Schacht, J., *Origins of Muḥammadan Jurisprudence* (Oxford: Oxford University Press, 1950).

Shackle, Christopher, and Stefan Speri, "Qaṣīda Poetry in Islamic Asia and Africa", 2 vols., in *Studies in Arabic Literature*, vol. 20 (Leiden: Brill, 1997).

Silverstein, A., *Postal-Systems in the Pre-Modern Islamic World: Cambridge Studies in Islamic Civilization* (New York: Cambridge University Press, 2007).

Speight, M., "A Look at Variant Readings in the *Ḥādīth*", *DI*, 77 (2000).

Stetkevych, Jaroslav, *Arabic Poetry and Orientalism* (Oxford: St John's College Research Centre, 2004).

Stetkevych, S., *Early Islamic Poetry and Poetics: The Formation of the Classical Islamic World* (Farnham, Surrey: Ashgate Variorum, 2009).

———, *The Mute Immortals Speak: Pre-Islamic Poetry and the Poetics of Ritual* (Ithaca, NY: Cornell University Press, 1993).

Stewart, Devin, "*Saj'* in the Qur'an: Prosody and Structure", *JAL*, 21 (1990).

Stroumsa, S., "The Blinding Emerald: Ibn al-Rawandī's *Kitab al-Zumurrud*", *JAOS*, 114 (1994).

________, "Ibn al-Rawandī's *Su' adab al-mujadala*: The Role of Bad Manners in Medieval Disputations" in H. Lazarus-Yaffe, et al. (eds.), *The Majlis: Interreligious Encounters in Medieval Islam, Studies in Arabic Language and Literature* (Wiesbaden: Harassowitz, 1999).

Taqqush, M. S., *Tārīkh al-dawla al-Umawīyya* (Beirut: Dār al-Nafā'is, 1996).

Thompson, Willie, *Postmodernism and History* (New York: Palgrave Macmillan, 2004).

Tyan, E., *Histoire de l'organisation judiciare en pays d'Islam* (Paris, 1938-1943; 2nd edition, Leiden, 1960) in Watt, W. Montgomery,"God's Caliph: Qur'ānic Interpretations and Umayyad Claims", *Iran and Islam*, ed. C.E. Bosworth (Edinburgh: Edinburgh University Press, 1971).

'Uways, Abd al-Ḥalīm, *Banū Umayyah bayn al-suqūt wa al-intiḥār; dirāsah ḥawl suqūṭ Banū Umayyah fī al-mashriq* (Cairo: Dār al-Sahwa, 1987).

al-Wakīl, Muḥammad al-Sayyid, *al-Umawīyun bayna al-sharq wal-gharb: dirāsah waṣfīyah wa-taḥlīlīyah lil-dawlah al-Umawīyah* (Damascus: Dār al-Qalam, 1995).

Walmand, M. R., *Toward a Theory of Historical Narrative* (Columbus: Ohio State University Press, 1980).

Watt, W. Montgomery, *The Formative Period of Islamic Thought* (Edinburgh: Edinburgh University Press, 1973).

________,"God's Caliph: Qur'ānic Interpretations and Umayyad Claims", *Iran and Islam*, ed. C.E. Bosworth (Edinburgh: Edinburgh University Press, 1971).

________, *Muḥammad at Mecca* (Oxford: Clarendon Press, 1953).

________, "Shī'ism under the Umayyads", *JRAS* (1960).

Wansborough, J., *Qur'ānic Studies: Sources and Methods of Scriptural Interpretation* (Oxford: Oxford University Press, 1977).

Weber, Max, *Max Weber on Charisma and Institution Building: Selected Papers*, ed. S.N. Eisenstadt (Chicago: University of Chicago Press, 1968).

Wellhausen, J., *The Arab Kingdom and its Fall*, tr. Margaret Weir (Beirut: Khayats, 1963).

________, *The Religio-Political Factions of Early Islam*, ed. R.C. Ostle, trans. R.C. Ostle and S.M. Waltzer (Amsterdam: North Holland Publishing, 1975).

White, Hayden, *Metahistory: The Historical Imagination in Nineteenth-Century Europe* (Baltimore: Johns Hopkins University Press, 1973).

Wolfson, H., *The Philosophy of the Kalam* (Cambridge, MA: Harvard University Press, 1976).

Appendix

عن مخشي بن حجر بن عدي عن ابيه ان نبي الله (ص) خطبهم فقال : اي يوم هذا؟ فقالوا: يوم حرام . قال : فاي بلد هذا؟ قالوا: بلد حرام , قال : فاي شهرهذا؟ قالوا: شهر حرام , قال : فان دماءكم واموالكم واعراضكم حرام عليكم كحرمة يومكم هذا, كحرمة شهركم هذا, كحرمة بلدكم هذا, ليبلغ الشاهد الغائب , لاترجعوابعدي كفارا يضرب بعضكم رقاب بعض

Source: المستدرك ج 3 / ص 470

شعيب بن حرب عن شعبة عن ابي بكر بن حفص عن حجر بن عدي رجل من اصحاب النبي (ص) عن النبي (ص) قال : ((ان قوما يشربون الخمر يسمونها بغير اسمها

Source: الاصابة ج 1 / ص 313.

حجر بن عدي الكندي قال : ((قلت لحجر: اني رايت ابنك دخل الخلاء ولم يتوضا, قال : ناولني الصحيفة من الكوة . فقرا: بسم الله الرحمن الرحيم ,هذا ما سمعت علي بن ابي طالب يذكر: ان الطهور نصف الايمان

Source: الطبقات ج 6 / ص 220.

((عن حجر انه قال : ((سمعت علي بن ابي طالب يقول : الوضوءنصف الايمان
وروى ابن عساكر ايضا باسناده الى حجر بن عدي قال : ((سمعت شراحيل بن مرة يقول :
((سمعت النبي (ص) يقول لعلي : ابشر يا علي , حياتك وموتك معي

Source: تاريخ ابن عساكر ج 4 / ص 85.

شريك قال : اخبرنا عبدالله بن سعد عن حجر بن عدي قال : قدمت المدينة فجلست الى ابي هريرة , فقال : ممن انت ؟ قلت : من اهل البصرة , قال : ما فعل سمرة بن جندب ؟, قلت : هو حي , قال : ما احد احب الي طول حياة منه , قلت : ولم ذاك ؟ قال : ان رسول (ص) قال لي وله ولحذيفة بن اليمان : ((آخركم موتافي النار), فسبقنا حذيفة , وانا الان اتمنى ان اسبقه , قال : فبقى سمرة بن جندب , حتى شهدمقتل الحسين((

Source: شرح نهج البلاغة ج 4 / ص 78.

More Titles by Dr. Sayed Ammar Nakshawani

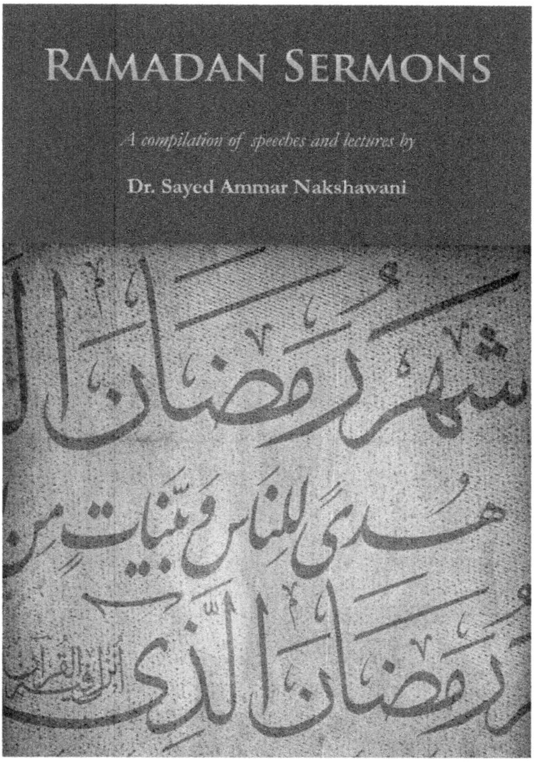

Ramadan Sermons is a compilation of thirty lectures delivered during the month of Ramadan around the world over the last ten years.

Transcribed and edited from audio lectures, this series addresses some of the most fundamental principles in Islam, in a clear and engaging manner. These include: the philosophies behind du'a and jihad; the reasoning behind the prohibition of alcohol and pork and a systematic approach to answering the question of whether the Holy Qur'an is the word of God.

"This book is a compilation of Dr. Sayed Ammar Nakshawani's lectures on the biographies of the fourteen infallible figures in Shi'a Islam. It is a very invaluable resource in that it presents these illustrious figures as representing and manifesting universal human values that can serve humanity at large. This excellent work also illustrates how they can serve as role models for all human beings."

Dr. Liyakat Takim, Sharjah Chair in Global Islam,
McMaster University, Canada